# The Plan of Record

# The Plan of Record

◆

## Producing Successful Computer Products Worldwide

*Wayne Holovacs, Ph.D., MBA, BS*

iUniverse, Inc.
New York  Lincoln  Shanghai

# The Plan of Record
## Producing Successful Computer Products Worldwide

iUniverse, Inc.

For information address:
iUniverse, Inc.
2021 Pine Lake Road, Suite 100
Lincoln, NE 68512
www.iuniverse.com

This publication is designed to provide accurate and authoritative information in regard to the subject matter covered. It is sold with the understanding that the publisher is not engaged in rendering legal, accounting, or other professional service. If legal advice or other expert assistance is required, the services of a competent professional should be sought.

ISBN: 0-595-29886-9 (pbk)
ISBN: 0-595-66071-1 (cloth)

Printed in the United States of America

# Contents

# FOREWORD

The POR details the process of setting in place a system of strategic Internet Personal Computer Product management and Quality Control plan, from the plan's inception in response to problems and hazards within the personal computer industry as a whole and Compaq Computer Corporation™ and three Subject Companies specifically, through its development, implementation, and finally through the assessment of its success based on consumer feedback, testing and measurement when implementation was finalized.

The Plan of Record (POR), Plan of Record Index (PORI) and Customer Satisfaction Index (CSI) are creations, under the auspices of Compaq Computer Corporation™ and three Subject Companies identified as D, H and I, the author and a Core Team of skilled professionals.

Beginning as a hobbyist industry, with components assembled on benches in enthusiasts' garages, the personal computer industry burgeoned rapidly as market demands made mass production essential. It was thus, initially, an out of control industry, undisciplined, with entrepreneurs gambling and often losing, with new companies springing up, prospering briefly, and then crashing, and with old. The more established companies making dangerous miscalculations. This background, as well as an overview of the current volatile nature of the industry, is presented through traditional research into available literature.

The premise for the Plan of Record (POR) and its accompanying instruments of measurement, the Plan of Record Index (PORI) and Customer Satisfaction Index (CSI) demonstrated that it is possible to identify those areas in the industry process (called Dependent Variables in this book) where lack of information invites chance, accident, miscalculation and failure—and, further, that a plan can be devised providing directions or instruments for doubling back, testing, analyzing and resolving issues that will supply the information necessary to avoid costly and ruinous errors, both in full-scale production and in customer satisfaction.

The methodology employed by the author and Core Team in developing this plan explains the methodology of the plan itself.

A unique feature of the Plan of Record (POR), which incorporates two previous, now inadequate plans, the SPC and TQC, is that it includes Customer Services and Consumer Response as an integral part of the industry process—not terminating company involvement with the boxed and shipped "final" product. Instead, invaluable feedback obtained through the PORI and CSI is automatically looped back to Planning and Design so that product improvement is immediate and ongoing. Because the PORI and CSI were in place, it was possible to measure the success of the Plan of Record (POR) at that stage of its initial implementation, and the results of those measurements are presented.

The results of these measurements indicate clearly that the Plan of Record (POR), with the accompanying instruments, the Plan of Record Index (PORI) and the Customer Satisfaction Index (CSI), constitute a highly effective tool for strategic Internet Personal Computer Product management and Quality Control.

In terms of the four companies studied, having the Plan of Record (POR) in place and in active implementation has a positive financial impact in all eight of the designated categories of measurement.

# ACKNOWLEDGEMENTS

To our Customers, Suppliers$^{TM}$/Vendors$^{TM}$, Compaq Computer Corporation$^{TM}$, the three Subject Companies specifically through its (POR) development, implementation, and finally through the assessment of its success based on customer/consumer feedback, testing, and measurement when implementation was finalized.

The Plan of Record (POR), Plan of Record Index (PORI) and Customer Satisfaction Index (CSI) are creations, under the auspices of Compaq Computer Corporation$^{TM}$ and three Subject Companies identified as D$^{TM}$, H$^{TM}$ and I$^{TM}$, the author and a Core Team of skilled professionals.

**Special thanks** are due to those who helped in the production of this book: My wife, Carol, my children, Benjamin, Nicholas, my mother, Mrs. Pauline Holovacs who taught me, "never-give-up" and do "what is right", and my Compaq and Supplier/Vendor family...all several thousand of them around the globe...

A heart-felt thank you to **Dr. W. Edwards Deming,** his works, teachings and all who continue to strive to create and move forward business management information technologies toward the greater good. **Dr. Deming** will always be remembered as "**The *Father of Quality***".

**Thanks** to those I never met but whose words and ideas somehow reached me. Acknowledgement is due to individuals whose names I cannot remember (or never recorded) yet who provided this author and the Core Team with essential help. People I met and spoke to during this research or while on the job, individuals whose questions or comments that helped clarify my own thoughts. My thanks go out to those individuals whose ideas and writings I criticize in this work as incorrect or limited in practice. I hope my criticism is taken in the manner intended—of free and open discussions of ideas so we all may obtain greater clarity. No personal affront is intended or implied.

# INTRODUCTION

**Historians** like to trace the modern computer through several centuries of slow and orderly evolution. From the relatively primitive abacus down to a more immediate ancestor, the sophisticated calculus, then to the mammoth mainframes and from them through recent "generations," each more technologically advanced than the one preceding it. **Such histories work**, up to a point, giving one the sense of a great idea that had its embryonic beginnings in ancient times and grew gradually and methodically until, in the last half or indeed the last quarter of the troubled Twentieth Century, it came finally to fruition when the world was ready to receive and be forever changed by it—for the changes wrought by computerization have been universal and profound.

However, there has been little that could be perceived as gradual or orderly about the emergence of the personal computer (PC), specifically; its history has been brief and tumultuous—and coping with the implications of this product, social and economic, intellectual and humanitarian, is still an overwhelming prospect.

The personal computer industry has been, and in many respects still remains, an undisciplined industry—and as such it poses threats with regard to economic stability, social and moral issues, law enforcement, intellectual integrity.

On the economic scene, which is the primary concern, the steady introduction of new technology, the fluctuating markets, and the inadequacy of methods of Product Business Management and Quality Control have encouraged energetic speculation and enticed entrepreneurs on the one hand and doomed them to failure on the other. The project, which is the subject of this study is an attempt to provide a kind of discipline that can ultimately achieve a degree of economic stability within and among the Computer companies that make up this energetic but nervous and volatile industry.

In their book, *Fire in the Valley: The Making of the Personal Computer* (2000), Paul Freiberger and Michael Swaine recount an episode that can serve as a starting point for understanding the nature of the personal computer industry. In June, 1975, Bob Marsh, an electronics expert and computer hobbyist, and Les Felsenstein, a designer of several microcomputer products, were working on what they called an "intelligent terminal" kit.

It would consist of a terminal with semiconductor circuitry inside of it that would perform certain display and keyboard decoding functions. They had a deal with *Popular Electronics* technical editor Les Solomon that he would give their product a cover story if they could finish it by press time.

The two men were working in Marsh's garage, at least at first, and as they worked, it eventually dawned on them that they were not just designing a terminal but a real computer and one of a sort not yet built—for theirs was a screen, a keyboard, and a computer all in one. (Such accidental creations were fairly commonplace in the early history of the personal computer; amateurish designers and builders assembled components without knowing for certain ahead of time how or if they would all come together.) They wondered if they could "pull it off," and the tension mounted when Les Solomon gave them a deadline of thirty days. Freiberger and Swaine tell the story: "Marsh kept the pressure on, and within 45 days of his initial discussion with Les Solomon, he had a circuit board. But Solomon had given the team a 30-day deadline, so as they neared completion, Marsh booked a flight to New York and informed a bleary-eyed Lee Felsenstein that he was going, too. They stuffed the Sol [the name they gave their device] into two brown paper bags and carried it with them on the plane.

"The demonstration for Solomon at *Popular Electronics* was an utter disaster." The thing just didn't work. They made what excuses they could and, feeling hopeless at this point, flew to an appointment at *Byte,* where the presentation was even more disastrous. Felsenstein, dead on his feet from the grueling work schedule, fell asleep during the *Byte* demonstration.

"Well-rested and back in California at his workbench, he quickly located the problem—a short circuit. Marsh promptly put Felsenstein back on a plane to New York to demonstrate a working Sol with strict instructions to not reveal that it was actually a *computer*" (Freiberger & Swaine, 132-33).

Such was the personal computer industry, even as late as 1975—two men working frantically, first in a garage and then in the loft of an office building, not realizing at first that the components they had assembled trying to come up with a better terminal actually amounted to a technologically advanced computer, hauling the hastily built and apparently not carefully tested prototype on an airline flight to New York, having it fail to function at two separate demonstrations, and then returning home to discover that the failure was due to a fairly minor problem.

What is amazing about this story and the approach to design, production and marketing that it reflects is that in less than a decade—by 1982—the industry had mushroomed, with many competing companies and large quantity production. Les Freed gives the following sales figures for that year: "the **Times/Sinclair**™ 1000—600,000; **Commodore**™ VIC-20—over 600,000; **Atari**™ and Atari 800—600,000; **Texas Instruments**™ **99/4A**—530,000; **TRS-80 Model III**—300,000; **Apple II Plus**—200,000; **IBM**™ PC—200,000; and **Osborne**™ **1**—55,000" (Freed, 7).

Furthermore, within less than another decade, the Internet and the World Wide Web opened up opportunities for a global market, and the demands on production were multiplied. However, despite rapid and sweeping changes in the industry, to a great extent—one might say, to an alarming extent—the original mind-set has persisted.

Research, experimentation and discovery continued, and the drive to come up with something new—now highly competitive and secretive rather than open and sharing as had been the case with early **PC hobbyists**—spurred the industry. There was still a strong tendency to gamble, to take chances, to move spontaneously, to "go with" a new technology or what seemed to be a new open market and "let the chips fall where they might."

The first personal computers had been assembled from kits, and it was just accepted that there would be inconsistencies, depending on the skills of the assembler. This approach did not work well with mass production, where duplication and repeatability were essential—nor did it work with consumers who were not computer hobbyists and who just wanted units to function as companies advertised they would. **At this stage in PC history**, there were too many unknowns. Computers were assembled from component parts: would suppliers be able to provide these components when mass production began? Would the designated prototype actually lend itself to duplication and to mass reproduction on the assembly line? Did the projected market PC exist? Or the opposite problem might arise: would demand far exceed production? Basically, **PC companies** had not developed systems for providing crucial information, and many **paid a heavy price**.

During the eighties and nineties, new companies sprang up, prospered briefly, and then folded; more established companies experienced severe set-backs due to unanticipated problems and miscalculations. It was a high-energy industry but a very dangerous one. Through the **80s** and early **90s**, two product management information systems were adopted by the PC industry in an attempt to bring order and uniformity to the production and marketing of the personal computer, first the SPC (Statistical Process Control) and then the TQC (Total Quality Control).

These product management information systems will be discussed at greater length during the course of this book.

In their efforts to implement SPC and TQC specifications and standards, companies like Compaq, the primary subject company in this book, had already begun to devote time, space and staff to pre-builds and small-scale manufacture—and some inroads had been carved with regard to understanding the nature and extent of consumer markets.

**But solutions were still inadequate**. For instance, fall-outs still numbered 100 out of every 1,000 units sent down the assembly line (multiply that by the hundreds of thousands of units involved in mass production, and it becomes obvious that the loss could be ruinous), and consumer response clearly indicated that "finished products" often failed to function as expected, or required extensive servicing.

**Then came the Internet** and the World Wide Web and the prospect of a global market. Was the PC industry ready for so great a challenge? The answer was, probably not.

In **1991** the introduction of the Internet ushered in a new technology, a world market, and a staggering array of existing and projected Internet consumer products. The global market place was changing, and along with it the global economy, as information of various kinds became increasingly electronic. As Stephen Barlas pointed out in 1996, "In the United States, U.S. companies feverishly seek Internet personal computer products that meet their company requirements"(Barlas, 70). "Feverishly" was an adverb aptly chosen. For in the PC industry the race was on, and no one was very certain about the rules. What personal computer manufacturing companies that expected to produce Internet personal computer products globally needed to do was not all that difficult to figure out. They had to meet global strategic market demands, they had to reduce computer manufacturing costs within all geographic regions, they had to decrease the cost of ownership to customers, they had to create standard Warranty and Configurable Warranty by allowing the customer a window of choice—but at the same time, ensure reduced Warranty costs. The question was not so much what broad industry goals must be met but how computer companies could go about trying to meet them. To some extent, these industry challenges had always existed, but they were greatly enhanced by the developing necessity of adequately addressing multiple market product features, like form, fit and function requirements, and product volume deliverables on a global basis.

**Gerald Page** correctly notes, in **1995**, "Personal computer manufacturers' strategic product management, strategic market planning, product concept, engineering, serviceability, development, assembling, and production controls became basic functions [with the introduction of the Internet] and needed to be integrated in the automatic factory" (Page, 64).

**Holmes, Randolph**, Brooks and Barry, writing in **1998**, are even more specific: "Strategic product management and market planning needs to be a top priority" (Holmes, *et. al.,* 16). And **Gene McCarroll**, also in **1998**, made the following summation: "In an economy increasingly dependent on information and technology, marketing ideas and creativity make up most of a company's wealth" (McCarroll, 10).

It was, in fact, generally acknowledged that effective planning and management were essential, not just at the marketing level, but in every phase of the industry process. It was likewise generally acknowledged that, though the management systems already in place, **SPC and the TQC, had effected improvements in the personal computer industry, they were inadequate** in terms both of the opportunities offered and of the economic dangers posed by the global market which was being opened up by the Internet and the World Wide Web. A strategic product management plan, more exact and comprehensive than the SPC and TQC, was needed to increase the business success of Internet personal computer product producers in the various categories of the production and marketing processes.

# Motivation For The Plan of Record

The foregoing discussion serves to establish the overall industry environment or context within which the problems that confronted Compaq Computer Corporation$^{TM}$, that arose during the late 1990s as well as with other suppliers/vendors partners globally.

A growing awareness of the seriousness of these problems, which emerged in all of the major areas of the computer industry process—design, manufacture, distribution and customer service—motivated the research examined and the development of the Plan of Record (POR) and its elements PORI and CSI.

In the area of PC design it was obvious that Compaq's product was becoming less reliable and that quality was dropping as was in this industry in general. These inadequacies were evidenced, first, by the rate of return per unit, which increased over a previous quarter worldwide, and, second, by the fact that the three major components—display, hard drive and mother board (PCA)—showed the highest failure rate to date, increasing consistently over time—an increase that was partly attributed to suppliers' inability to test parts accurately before shipping to Compaq$^{TM}$.

Manufacturing and Quality in the broad area of manufacturing and the quality, within the finished product, a rash of customer complaints was noticed over a two-quarter period. Products were not meeting customer expectations with regard to functionality as well as with regard to company response to customer feedback. Customer Service limitations in terms of customer feedback had became obvious that the company lacked a comprehensive method of operation for providing answers and effective remedies when product failures were reported. What was the problem? Simply stated, *Compaq and its supplier/vendor base as well as the PC industry as a whole had a limited system process in place* that facilitated unclear communication among the separate phases of the industry process: design, supplier partnerships, manufacturing, distribution and customer feedback.

Addressing these mounting concerns, especially as they affected and were tied in with the marketing and servicing end of the industry process, was and still is a responsibility of management.

It became mandatory that research and assessment be instigated, first to determine the causes of the problems that were arising in all major areas of the industry process and then to make some informed projections as to what should be involved in developing a plan, or set of procedures, or system that would eliminate or avert these failures in each step of the product's manufacture.

Certain questions presented themselves. Questions arose in the area of design, the question was, were the engineers designing products to meet market needs with regard to newest technology, display characteristics, power requirements and ease of use? In the area of manufacturing, a number of questions required answering: Were manufacturing processes documented and updated? Were the Assembler's properly trained and was their training documented? At the end of the manufacturing line, was there a quality engineer on station to pass or fail each unit?

# Marketing, Distribution, Customer Service

A question that often arose in the areas of Marketing and Distribution was still a nagging concern: Was Compaq shipping a sufficient quantity of units to supply the market within each region globally?

In the area of Customer Service, the main question was a simple one: Did Compaq have a good understanding of what customers wanted? Closely related to that general question was a more definite point of inquiry: was some provision, some tool, in place that made it possible for customer response to the finished product at the end of the industry process to feed back into design at the beginning of the industry process, thus identifying customer concerns and product issues and insuring that they would be noted and corrected and enhanced features put into place?

Furthermore, in connection with serving customers effectively, was there a documented process for contacting customers in the event of significant failures and guidelines for how Compaq would take action?

Systems Analysis began a comprehensive systems analysis was initiated and conducted at two levels of scope and intensity. A cursory analysis was effected prior to presenting a proposal for the development and implementation of a new process plan to senior management; once the proposal was approved and the Core Team appointed, a systems analysis of a much broader scope and greater detail was an ongoing part of the program for developing and implementing the proposed plan. Then with the assistance of the appointed team, reviewed failure percentages, records of units shipped, and component test processes identified specific customer feedback for form, fit and function per unit and visited manufacturing sites worldwide, identifying and reviewing each step of the industry process as workers at each site built the units specified.

For reasons of confidentiality, all raw data in this book are classified making it impossible to give exact findings resulting from either the cursory or extended systems analysis. [However, it can be stated that at each stage of the industry process, both in this country and abroad, inadequacies were significant enough to justify the on-the-site research that had been proposed and the development of a plan that would identify and provide a system for correcting problems during the industry process and thus insure that a quality product would come off of the assembly line and be strategically marketed and effectively serviced globally.]

Consequently, the systems analysis narrowed the questions for research and development to two essential issues: (1) Could the team identify the distinct points or junctures within each phase of the industry process where a lack of information or misinformation resulted in accidents, miscalculations, fallouts and financial loss? (These would become the Dependent Variables in the POR) (2) Was it possible to design and implement a plan, a comprehensive testing and measurement tool that would provide the information necessary to avoid failures and glitches in the industry process and the financial instability that resulted from them? These two questions comprised the problem that would be addressed through research.

# The Hypothesis

Research aimed at developing what would become the POR (Plan of Record) was based on the **hypothesis** that it is possible, first, to identify and single out those areas in the personal computer industry process where a lack of information resulted in accidents, miscalculations, errors, and ultimately fallout and financial loss. The Core Team decided to call these areas in which the elements of chance and guess-work had previously prevailed "**Dependent Variables**". It was further hypothesized that a carefully devised and implemented system of testing, measurement, double-checking and attention to feedback could provide sufficient information to bring such areas into an acceptable degree of conformity and predictability and greatly minimize the factors of chance and accident.

Computerization helped, **computerization** itself made designing such a system or plan possible and feasible. Vast amounts of data can be collected, stored, analyzed, and transmitted quickly and easily. It was a part of the hypothesis that the new strategic product management tool could incorporate the historical methods, the Statistical Process Control and Total Quality Control and go beyond them to encompass the greater complexities of planning, developing and marketing personal computer and Internet computer products globally.

# The Purpose of POR-PORI-CSI

The point was made in the foregoing discussion that the POR (Plan of Record) and the PORI (Plan of Record Index) have been developed beyond the hypothetical stage and are now concrete creations capable of being implemented and assessed in terms of their results.

Thus far, the POR-PORI-CSI had been utilized specifically by Compaq and other suppliers/vendors and OEM companies, also vendors and suppliers, directly associated with Compaq. This demonstrates that the strategic product management plan, the POR complemented by the index PORI, and CSI (Customer Service Index) has helped those companies achieve production and marketing goals, reducing miscalculations, fallout, shutdowns and the loss in time and material that they represent and, thus, increasing profit well beyond expectations.

It is likewise the intent of this book to suggest that other Internet personal computer product producers would benefit from implementing the Plan of Record (POR), which would enable them to avoid trial and error attempts to address problem's that are similar to those encountered by Compaq and the Subject Companies in which the plan was implemented.

# Definition of Terms You May Not Know

Gate Process. Agreement to Continue Decision path to set aside resolving an issue by moving the open gate into the next phase with an increased priority level.

A-Level Gate. Most critical completion requirement. Violation of this gate will most likely result in significant reduction in customer quality and/or factory capacity levels.

Bill of Material (BOM). List of materials, soft goods, parts that are required to build a unit or software package.

Build to Order (BTO). For the purpose of the POR, Build to Order is intended to represent the retail market (Best Buy, Sears, these are channel partners) personal computer product.

B-Level Gate. Violation of this gate will most likely result in less efficient use of resources, slower ramp times, etc.

C-Level Gate. Violation of this gate will result in delayed schedules, less efficient use of resources, etc., but at an impact level that can be resolved by the Core Team, and is not expected to impact other programs or require POR modification.

Configure to Order (CTO). Configure to Order (CTO) is intended to represent the customer calling in a customer order by way of the telephone or Internet Web Site.

Corp. Ops. Team. Members decided by Corporate Operations Planning Program Manager, but should include as a minimum for this process: Corporate Operations Engineering, Manufacturing Site Engineering, Site Planning and Program Management.

Core Team. Members decided by appropriate Product Division Program Manager, and includes but is not limited to: Product Development, Corporate Operations Engineering, and Corporate Operations Planning, including, but not limited to, the Corporate Operations Planning Program Manager.

Escalate. Decision path to move issue to higher authority level for decision/direction.

First Pass Fallout (FPF) Gate. Determine line failure rate. Required completion level for Operations to successfully proceed.

Industrial Design. The form, fit, and function of the chassis, bezel and bucket.

Internal Unit Request (IUR). Units required by development teams to complete their evaluation.

Internet Personal Computer (IPC). Internet Personal Computer is intended to represent a personal computer that has the capability to access the Internet.

Life Cycle Model. Determine the life of the product.

Manufacturing Readiness. A measurement of the status of a program in terms of criteria, which need to be assessed throughout new product introduction phases. New product phases include: Design, System Integration, Product Validation, Manufacturing Verification, Ramp, and Volume.

Manufacture Verification Build (MVB). Build pre-production units to determine issues prior to production build.

Plan of Record. This document defines the operating parameters within which the Project Team and Core Team must execute to successfully deliver the company goals.

Plan of Record Index.(PORI) Plan of Record Index refers to a methodology that identifies key categories, variables to be examined per unit build plan worldwide.

Ramp Start of assembly through manufacturing process, until each unit meets volume expectation.

<u>Resolve.</u> Decision path to either complete the gate item, or to correct the issue associated with the gate and validate it as complete before advancing to the next phase, as well as modifying the POR if necessary.

<u>Roadmap.</u> Product document that forecasts specific product type and features.

<u>Statistical Process Control.</u> (SPC) Refers to statistical methodology and processes as measured per unit.

<u>Total Quality Control.</u> (TQC) Refers to product quality processes and the commitment of Senior Management.

# Technology Limitations

When surveying the literature on computer product strategic management for producing Internet personal computer product globally, quite aside from the more progressive fringe, one is impressed by the paucity of documentation. What does exist, are a few specialized books for specific and isolated tasks. Although these books provide a wealth of information on SPC (Statistical Process Control), and SPC (Simplified), they were considered redundant material. Statistical Process Control. (George Rosenwelg, 1988); Statistical Quality Control Handbook. (Western Electric Company, 1956); and Guide to Quality Control. (Ishikawa, 1982).

# The Empirical Research

Involved in developing and implementing the Plan of Record (POR) and its key components PORI and CSI was specific to Compaq Computer Corporation and three Subject Companies, designated as D, H and I (vendors, suppliers, etc. working in the Compaq community). The members of the POR development Core Team were experienced and knowledgeable with regard to trends, practices, methods and problems that existed in the overall industry and were, as a result, able to make informed generalizations in that regard—but direct, hands-on participation and observation was constrained by the boundaries of the four companies listed above. [Note that with the exception of Compaq, company names are confidential.]

These companies were identified in order to assess the value of Marketing, Production, Service, Operations and Customer Satisfaction using a Customer Satisfaction Index attribute data model (CSI).

[Caution should be used in generalizing the results of the rating methodology to the use of customer satisfaction as it relates to product quality.]

The POR development Core Team also reviewed E-Commerce Capabilities, Services Marketing, Product Warranty, Configurable Warranty, (OLS) On-Line Services, and Internet Keyboard. Correspondence, documents and various other raw data that are classified as confidential and cannot be specified in this study; however, the information obtained from examination of these materials is included in assumptions, conclusions, percentages and final figures that are included. [The product examples, Program and Project code names have also been changed to protect confidentiality.]

# Reviewing Current Literature
# The Need For Strategic Computer
# Product Management

The decision to design and implement the Plan of Record (POR), which is the subject of this book, evolved from on-the-scene observation and hands-on participation and experience in the computer industry. However, a substantial body of literature is available—books, articles, pamphlets, Internet websites—that provides context within which the need for such a plan can be understood.

Familiarity with the history of the computer is essential to comprehending the nature of the product and the industry that has burgeoned around it. Such historical accounts are plentiful and, as a general rule, differ from each other primarily in terms of which aspect of the industry, or sometimes which computer company, is the focus of their inquiry and assessment.

To the uninformed public it has seemed, perhaps, that the computer appeared rather suddenly on the scene in the late 1950s or early 1960s, multiplied and diversified dramatically over the next four decades, and fundamentally changed the way people interact, do business and obtain information. Computer historians point out that, quite the contrary, the modern computer is the result of centuries of human invention.

# History of The Computer

In *Computers: History and Development* (1994) Christopher LaMorte and John Lilly suggest that the abacus, which emerged about 5,000 years ago in Asia Minor, was the first computer.

LaMorte and Lilly trace the evolution of the computer through the invention of calculators by Blaise Pascal (in 1643) and Gottfried William von Leibniz (in 1694).

The real beginnings of computers as we know them today, according to LaMorte and Lilly and most other historians, lay with an English mathematics professor, Charles Babbage, who in 1822 proposed a machine to perform differential equations, called a Difference Machine.

Babbage's steam-powered Engine, although ultimately never constructed, outlined the basic elements of a modern general purpose computer and was a breakthrough concept (LaMorte & Lilly, 1-2).

As do other historians, LaMorte and Lilly divide the history of modern computers into five "generations." First Generation computers (1945–1956) were the products of increased government interest and funding during the Second World War, among them a secret code-breaking computer called the **Colossus** and an all-electric calculator produced to create ballistic charts for the U. S. Navy. The latter, called the Mark I for short, was an electronic relay computer and was about half the length of a football field and contained about 500 miles of wiring. Other computers spurred by the war were general-purpose computers, the Electronic Numerical Integrator and Computer (ENIAC), a piece of machinery so massive that it consumed 160 kilowatts of electrical power, and the Electronic Discrete Variable Automatic Computer (EDVAC) with a memory to hold both a stored program as well as data.

A key element of the EDVAC was the central processing unit, which allowed all computer functions to be coordinated through a single source. In 1951 the UNIVAC™ (Universal Automatic Computer), built by Remington Rand, became one of the first commercially available computers to take advantage of these advances (LaMorte & Lilly, 1-3). Stephen White, in *A Brief History of Com-*

*puters* (1996), notes that the next step in the history of computing was the invention of the transistor in 1947.

This replaced the inefficient valves with a much smaller and more reliable component. Large rooms filled with vacuum tubes were no longer necessary elements of computer construction and operation.

Transistorized computers are usually referred to as Second Generation and dominated the late 1950s and early 1960s—but despite certain advances in technology, they were still bulky and strictly used by universities and government. Jack St. Claire Kilby's invention, the integrated circuit or microchip—produced in 1958 but not appearing in computers until 1963—issued in the Third Generation and an explosion in the use of computers. As White notes, "While large 'mainframes' such as the **IBM 360** increased storage and processing capabilities further, the integrated circuit allowed the development of Microcomputers that began to bring computing into many smaller businesses" (White, 1).

# Nature of The Personal Computer Industry

Of particular interest to this research is the energetic and, in most ways, frantic and disorganized period of transition during which Fourth Generation computers made their appearance and began to grab a large share of the computer market. Needless to say, advances in technology ushered in this highly competitive era. For years, IBM$^{TM}$ had dominated the computer market with its big expensive mainframes. These huge, costly machines appealed to a dependable and fairly predictable group of consumers—organizations and businesses with enough cash to pay for the kind of help that the cumbersome mainframes offered. Even so, there was often a disparity between production and marketing.

For instance, **IBM's** most successful salesman of mainframe computers, **H. Ross Perot**, left the company to form Texas Instruments when he found himself consistently selling more computers than IBM was able to produce. Such disjunctures were frequent during this period from the late 1970s through the 1980s, which bristled with increasingly sophisticated technology and aroused public interest.

**Les Freed**, in "Personal Computers: History and Development," a chapter in his book, *The History of Computers* (1995), notes that "Until 1971, nobody even thought of a computer as anything but a big, fast, electronic brain that resided in a climate-controlled room and consumed data and electricity in massive quantities" (Freed, 3). Freed goes on to chronicle some of the technical advances that, as mentioned above, motivated the transition from Third Generation to Fourth Generation computers.

In **1971** the hand-held calculator was born when an **Intel 4004 chip** containing 4004 transistors was programmed to perform complex mathematical calculations by **1972**, teams of experts at **Intel, Digital Equipment Corporation**$^{TM}$ **(DEC) and Xerox**$^{TM}$ were actually working on and were reasonably successful in designing what could have become the first personal computers, Significantly, in all these cases management saw no value to the product and halted its development.

As Freed states: "In the end, none of the giant companies whose names had been synonymous with computers would introduce the **PC** to the world. There seemed to be no future in an inexpensive product that would replace the million dollar "**Big Iron**" that they were selling as fast as they could make them" (Freed, 3). Freed points out that "The people who eventually introduced **the PC were rebels.** "Just who these rebels were and why the early development of the personal computer depended upon them is engagingly detailed in a very readable book, *Fire in the Valley: The Making of the Personal Computer* (2000) by Paul Freiberger and Michael Swaine.

This book is an excellent means of "**getting the feel**" of the personal computer industry in its beginnings—the brilliant leaps forward, the set-backs, the often desperate competition and the intrigue. Since understanding this period in computer history sheds considerable light on the conditions that made designing and implementing the POR a necessity in terms of PC design, production and marketing, the Freiberger-Swaine book is a valuable resource. **In the first place**, Freiberger and Swaine examine the myopic thinking about production and marketing that influenced the large computer companies to reject the possibility of manufacturing small, relatively inexpensive PCs.

"**The marketing people**...explained that it [the popularity of the **handheld calculator**] was a matter of packaging. If someone wanted to do only calculations, they didn't want to have to fire up a computer to run a calculator program. Besides, most people, even scientists were intimidated by computers. A calculator was just a calculator from the moment you turned it on.

**A computer** was an instrument from the **Twilight Zone**" (Freiberger & Swaine, 16). Two factors had always complicated the production and marketing of computers, and these factors were particularly relevant to the proposed personal computers—computers were built from components that had to be secured from a variety of sources *and* they were not specific in terms of use or function.

The large computer companies could not visualize any segment of the population from which *consumers* were likely to be attracted to the product, i.e. they did not anticipate a use or function that the small computers might perform that would interest the general public in buying them.

**Many** of the "**rebels**" who wound up introducing the **PC** to the **world** had spent time working for the big companies and were frustrated by the lack of vision they encountered. They retreated into their own garages and attended meetings with other "computer nuts" who saw a much different future than the one laid out over the previous years by the giants of the computer industry. **The first PC was actually a "kit" for the Altair 8800**, sold by Micro Instrumentation and Telemetry Systems, Inc$^{TM}$. (**MITS**) beginning in the early 70s, that enabled **computer hobbyists** to assemble their own computers. It had no monitor, no keyboard, no printer, and couldn't store data, but the demand for it was overwhelming. Although rife with problems and limitations, the Altair helped launch one of the largest companies in the computer world, for **in 1974** Bill Gates and Paul Allen wrote a version of BASIC for the Altair and started a company called **Microsoft Corporation**$^{TM}$. **Then in 1976,** another computer kit was sold to hobbyists, the Apple I. Stephen Wozniak and Steve Jobs got together enough money to start Apple.

In **1977**, they introduced the **Apple II**, a pre-assembled PC with a color monitor, sound, and graphics. Even though the kits were popular, they were regarded as just a hobby, and Apple II was seen as a toy.

Freiberger and Swaine provide what might be termed an ethnographic description of the computer "hobbyist" culture which is worth examining in detail because it explains why no system of control or uniformity with regard to design, production, quality, marketing or customer service existed—and why introducing such systems has been an essential but difficult and often unsuccessful process.

For instance, these authors point out: "The Altair$^{TM}$ from MITS breached the machine room door, and rivals emerged almost all at once from garages all over the country. ...**But** commercial success was deemed irrelevant to the kindling of the revolution. Those who failed did so openly, with their schematics laid on the table for all to see.

Mistakes proved instructive, and failures did little to discourage increased innovation. The revolution was running on its own internal drive, and not according to the external pull of profits. The industry did not take shape according to traditional economic laws" (Freiberger & Swaine, 78). Freiberger and Swaine go on to explain: "The hobbyists were designing computers for themselves. Even the appearance of the machines reflected their hobbyist origins.

*The typical computer resembled a homemade piece of electronic test equipment*—a metal box rigged with toggle switches, blinking lights, and wires running out of its back, front, top and sides—a real 'kludge,' as computers made up of a hodge-podge of parts came to be called." "No one," they continue, "gave much thought to a machine's visual appeal because designers were creating the computers *they* wanted, regardless of how the end product looked" (Freiberger & Swaine, 80)

Even as this evolving PC industry grew and multiplied, it continued to run on enthusiasm and high energy and to be "out of control": "[T]he competition was heavy...The open trading of information, the shirt-sleeve management, the flashes of idealism, and the lack of detailed planning that had characterized the industry from the start still existed. But there was a growing belief that professional management may have its advantages; however, scarcely anyone considered it the time to put such a radical idea into practice. The chief users, designers, and company presidents were still hobbyists at heart, and most of the world knew nothing of the revolution that was afoot" (Freiberger & Swaine, 149). New companies were sprouting like mushrooms overnight, and their proliferation suggests both the contagious energy of the PC revolution and the mayhem among the revolutionaries. **Among the computer and computer-related companies in business at the end of 1977 were:** Apple Computer$^{TM}$ (which some insiders thought had great promise), Exidy$^{TM}$, IMSAL$^{TM}$, Digital Microsystems$^{TM}$, Alpha Micro Systems$^{TM}$, Commodore$^{TM}$, Midwest Scientific$^{TM}$, GNAT$^{TM}$, Southwest Technical Products$^{TM}$, MITS$^{TM}$, Technical Design Labs$^{TM}$, Vector Graphic$^{TM}$, Ithaca Audio$^{TM}$, Heathkit$^{TM}$, Cromemeo$^{TM}$, MOS Technology$^{TM}$, RCA$^{TM}$, TEI$^{TM}$, Ohio Scientific$^{TM}$, The Digital Group$^{TM}$, Micromation$^{TM}$, Polymorphic Systems$^{TM}$, Parasitic Engineering$^{TM}$, Godbout Engineering$^{TM}$, Radio Shack$^{TM}$, Dynabite$^{TM}$, North Star$^{TM}$, Morrow's Microsoft$^{TM}$, and, of course, Processor Technology$^{TM}$.

**In 1981**, as Freed recounts, two events occurred that served to validate the PC. In 1980 IBM$^{TM}$ had started a secret project in Boca Raton, Florida called Acorn and in 1981 introduced the **IBM PC**, a product that validated the PC as a legitimate business tool worthy of respect. According to Freed, "When the IBM PC hit the market, it was a complete system.

**Secretly, IBM** had provided software developers with prototypes of their PC so they could develop an array of programs that would be available when the machine hit the streets. IBM$^{TM}$ also developed printers, monitors, and expansion cards for the PC, and made it an open system so other manufacturers could develop peripherals for it". Freed goes on to note that "The IBM PC used an Intel$^{TM}$ **8088 microprocessor**, had 16K of RAM, was expandable to 256K, came with one 5.25-inch disk drive and room for a second, and was available with a choice of operating systems" (Freed, 5). The second major event of 1981 was, of course, the introduction of the first luggable computer, the Osborne 1. Incidentally, over the next two years, the **Osborne Computing Company**$^{TM}$ would go from nothing to a company with $70 million in annual revenue and then into bankruptcy. As has been stated, two factors have complicated the production and marketing of personal computers: the fact that they are assembled from components that must be obtained from a variety of suppliers and the fact that they cannot be advertised as having one particular use or function (like the hand-held calculator, for example).

**Ironically**, companies who have accommodated these two factors have fared much better than those that have attempted to "cover those bases." The Apple II computer, as has been stated, was regarded as a mere toy because its functions were limited and specific. In connection with components, it is significant that the highly successful IBM PC was an open system, which allowed other manufacturers to develop peripheral components that were compatible with the IBM machine.

In *Roadblocks on the Information Highway,* Charles E. Gardner calls attention to An Wang, a technical genius and innovator, who introduced the WANG™ 2200 in the mid l970s. Unlike other PCs of the era, which as has been mentioned looked like they were patched together in someone's basement, the **WANG™ 2200 and the WANG OIS** that followed had solid one-piece metal construction with the screen and keyboard in the same console and, with their tastefully muted colors, looked like they belonged in offices, banks and brokerages. But WANG™ replaced the enhanced BASIC programming capability with a turn-key word processing system and tightened the proprietary leash on its customers by making cable and interface alterations to industry standard printers and disks it purchased from other vendors to make it impossible for **WANG** owners to purchase and connect other brands of equipment to a WANG system. Though the WANG system enjoyed some initial popularity, the company soon faltered (Gardner, 1-2). It is noted in the Smart Computing Editorial, "The Rise Of The 'Wintel Monopoly'," that "The success of the IBM PC and the growth of the entire personal computer industry took everyone by surprise, including IBM.

By 1984, three out of every four personal computers sold were IBM PCs. Other PC manufacturers jumped on the bandwagon, designing computers that were compatible with IBM's. Because IBM had gone outside for the most important components of the computer—the microprocessor and operating system—other companies could purchase the same products from Microsoft™ and Intel to make clones of the PC that would run the same software.

The **editorial goes** on to conclude "The proliferation of **IBM-compatibles** had several lasting effects on the growing PC industry. Non-IBM-compatible systems all but disappeared, as software and hardware manufacturers concentrated on the new standard. Only Apple still survives" ("Wintel Monopoly,"1).

The fact that the possibilities of the PC and the obvious growing market for it finally convinced big computer companies like IBM to begin developing their own products validated the product and the industry. Nevertheless, the PC industry was still in many respects **a "run away,"** an industry that in its beginnings had not conformed to traditional economic laws. This aspect of the industry soon created problems for both management and consumers. Robert T. and David M. Amsden and Howard E. Butler explained "As computer companies began to manufacture with limited information about transportable computers, manufacturing and marketing processes, planning and product management standards needed to be identified quickly."

# Statistical Process Control &
# Total Quality Control

Their book, *SPC Simplified*, outlines and clarifies the first of two product management information systems that were devised in attempts to regulate and facilitate the production and marketing of the PC.

The system that these authors discuss is Statistical Process Control (SPC). As they note, "Statistical Process Control (SPC) methods assist the planning and product management processes" (Amsden & Butler, 100). While Statistical Process Control (SPC) worked to alleviate some of the problems in the PC industry, the system could not anticipate the rapid changes brought about by steadily increasing, ever more sophisticated technology.

**The manufacturing challenges** were great as companies struggled to meet the demands of growing and often unexpected markets—and of consumers who, unlike the first PC enthusiasts, were no longer willing to tolerate shortcomings and glitches and who were savvy enough to see possibilities that had not been realized and to demand that these be incorporated in their product. In an article titled "Product Management," published in the April 1989 edition of *Quality*, Anthony Costanzo insisted, "Research is needed to understand and meet the larger market demands for a higher quality personal computer product" (Costanzo, 23).

**Computer companies struggled** to meet this challenge. This new research produced an information technology strategic product management, marketing tool called Total Quality Control (**TQC**). Complying with this process would clearly identify the manufacturing facility as meeting the high standards that the market demanded, assuring that a company was a **World-Class manufacturer.** Within a few years, however, it became obvious that neither of the strategic management information technologies discussed above provided the documentation and structure needed to hold market gains. Personal computer manufacturing companies globally were unable to meet strategic marketing and company goals.

As a result of failing to develop a new strategic product management information technology that would enable them to meet market demand and company goals, many computer manufacturers went out of business.

As **Larry E. Geisel** states in "Knowledge-Based CIM Support," published in **** *Manufacturing Systems,* "In 1995 personal computer manufacturing producers and management stages, planning, concept, engineering, serviceability, development, assembling, and product controls would be the basic function to be integrated in the automatic factory" (Geisel, 11).

The fact was that another major development was affecting the already volatile personal computer industry. Jason Thomas, in a chapter titled "Reactions by the Computer Industry to the World Wide Web" from his book *Ethics and Law on the Electronic Frontier* (1994), analyzes the impact of the Internet and the World Wide Web on the computer industry. States Thomas, "Spurred by the current popularity of the World Wide Web (WWW) computer users are flocking to the Internet., [F]or the computer industry, the WWW provides limitless opportunity. The **computer industry has taken notice** of this opportunity, and is rushing to create services that satisfy this market of computer oriented consumers" (Thomas, 1), Thomas takes a positive and enthusiastic view of the possibilities of the Internet and the WWW for the computer industry, though he does admit that many of the on-line services previously provided by computer companies are "showing their age."

**He insists** that the "bottom line" for computer companies is that "They can provide access to all members of the Internet for a cost comparable to supporting forums on a single on-line service. No more headaches over deciding which on-line service to base their operations from. **No need** to finance the on-line connect time to lure customers to their forums, etc." (Thomas, 2). All this sounds well and good, and as Stephen Barlas notes in *Managing Automation,*

"New computer products were being introduced into the market place at a fast pace, U. S. companies feverishly were seeking Internet Personal Computer products" (Barlas, 70).

Unfortunately, the "**sky is the limit**" possibilities opened up by the Internet and the WWW and the "feverish" pace at which computer products were and are being introduced in the industry have their downsides.

In between the **grand visions** for the possibilities for personal computers and the concrete realization of those visions is a murky area that happy dreamers like Jason Thomas hardly acknowledge: frustrations and setbacks at the design table, shortages of necessary components, inefficient assembly lines, unexpected slumps or surges in consumer demand, problems with moving merchandise, mounting complaints from consumers—and, of course, relentless competition. Larry K. Geisel sums up the problem: "Manufacturing operations, workforce planning, strategy, and redundant product qualifications regardless of the degree of automation, are integrated only by expert human intelligence. Although computer integration manufacturing (CIM) objectives are simply that this expertise—the value added—can be automated to integrate factory operations, one must ask where value is being added in the current operation" (Geisel, 11, 56-57). **John Harvey and Gerald L. Page**, in a **1997** *Harvard Business Review* **article**, are even more explicit in designating the problem, "Smaller US and international manufacturers are caught between pressure from customers for improved quality and delivery and the pressure of increased competition. Manufacturers are faced with the choice of improving manufacturing operations or closing" (Harvey & Page, 72).

It can be reasonably argued that, to a considerable extent, these factors apply to larger companies, as well, and that improving marketing and customer service is equally essential.

# Current Problems In The Personal Computer Industry

As has been demonstrated, a review of the books and articles that examine the history of the computer—and the personal computer (PC) in particular—provides insight as to why this industry, which began with hobbyists working in their garages and grew rapidly and un-expectedly, did not initially develop a procedure for computer product management, why attempts to develop such procedures have not been as effective as they need to be, and **why**, with the advent of the **Internet** and **WWW**, a procedure such as the **Plan of Record (POR)** is absolutely essential in order for companies to meet strategic market demands, reduce manufacturing costs, and increase customer satisfaction. Other literature that supports the argument that the Plan of Record (POR) is a much-needed and, as yet, generally unavailable tool consists of articles in various trade and business Journals and on the Internet.

[It should be kept in mind that the articles examined here may or may not deal specifically with the issues with which the originators of the POR were themselves confronted; much of the material made available to the POR team is protected by policies pressure that exists at the Design and Production and Manufacturing level.]

A good lead-off article is Roberta Faletra's "Is there no one willing to shake it up in this industry any longer?" published in the May 7, 2001 issue of *CRN: The Newsweekly for Builders of Technology Solutions*. As Falenta's title indicates, she is impatient for something new. **She challenges** the computer industries: "Maybe the rut we are in is due to a lack of vendor leadership or a willingness to simply stir things up."

Falenta complains, "When I look out a few months down the line, there is no major new introduction we are all waiting on," and she notes nostalgically, "I'll never forget **the buzz** that surrounded some of the truly groundbreaking introductions of the past"—she mentions the Macintosh™, Windows 3.0, Lotus Notes™, and others. She concludes, "I'm afraid the big players are too big and for some reason they think they can survive no matter what happens"(Falenta,

140-1) Falenta is a journalist, and she seems as concerned about the absence of PR hype as she is about the absence of new inventions, but she embodies the kind of pressure imposed on computer companies and to which they must respond in order to survive.

Several articles call attention to innovations in the computer industry, to the kind of scrutiny to which such innovations or inventions are subjected, and to the mixed receptions they often receive. Robert A. Guth and Evan Ramstad are authors of a *Wall Street Journal* article,

"How **Sony Turned a Skinny Laptop Into** an Unlikely PC System" (**Nov. 12, 1999**). Picking up on the word "Unlikely" in their title, Guth and Ramstad begin their article, "Computer industry veterans chuckled when Sony Corp. unveiled the Vaio, its purple personal computer, in 1996." They go on to recount that the Vaio survived, and they credit its survival to the fact that "They [Sony] perceived ahead of everybody else a change in consumer buying trends" (Guth & Ramstad, B, 1-2). In "Textbook notebook," an article in the **April 16, 2001** issue of *Brandweek,* Todd. Wesserman comments on **Hewlett-Packard's introduction of its Pavilion** consumer notebook product, Though the Pavilion was selling reasonably well, Wesserman makes some significant comments about **Hewlett-Packard's troubles** with their products: "HP followed its initial success with price cuts calculated to undercut rivals while generating enough margin to keep retailers happy. Things did not always go smoothly. HP's Pavilion PCs sold well, but were often in short supply. Aping the model of then-market leader Packard Bell[TM], **HP released too many Pavilion SKUs** at first and later pared them back. **Despite such mishaps**, by 1998, HP was vying with Compaq at retail for No. 1 in desktop PCs....Then retailers began asking when HP was going to release a consumer Note: book"—though at the time the market was lagging and only 20% of notebooks were sold through retail (18-20).

Wasserman's comments highlight the problems such as production not keeping up with demand or flooding the market, problems that a strong and effective system of product control would help to eliminate. Wasserman writes another *Brandweek* article. "Softness yields CE focus for PC vets, Microsoft plans two lines of attack," dated January 15, 2001, in which he reports that several PC **industry veterans, Microsoft[TM], Compaq[TM], Intel[TM]** and **Hewlett-Packard[TM]**, are attempting to crash into computer electronics because there are signs of a slowdown in the PC industry (Wesserman, 14). In an article, "Virtual assembly processes come to the PC screen," published in *Design News,* April 19, 1999, Laurie Ann Toupin comments that Adept Technology's[TM] development of a 3D CAD reflects that "Emphasis in the computer-aided design-tool market seems to be shifting from product management to process management and from individual components to assemblies" (Toupin, 18).

**Ira Sager's** article, **"Bringing Mainframe Might to PC Servers,"** in *Business Week*, **July 5, 1999**, focuses on the strategy by which **IBM is "winning back customers and giving competitors fits**." Sager notes that "In order to get past rivals, IBM has given its PC servers a complete technology overhaul while pumping up its marketing…The key makeover ingredient: putting the best of its mainframe know-how and reliability into the smaller, cheaper machines" (Sager, 88).

[The above articles are current but are not arranged chronologically simply because chronology is not relevant and the events do not follow a cause and effect line of progression. The articles convey the nature of the personal computer industry—the powerful pressure to be constantly coming out with innovative machinery and software, the intense competition, the unpredictable twists and turns of the market, and the (too often, completely unexpected and unprepared for) failures and successes of various products.]

**Interestingly**, three of the articles included in this study deal with natural disasters in Taiwan. As has been noted, the fact that computers are assembled from components provided by a variety of suppliers has always been a factor that computer companies have had to cope with at the production and manufacturing level.

**Taiwan** is an important manufacturer of computer components such as semiconductors, memory chips, etc. Therefore, **an earthquake in September** of 1999 and a **typhoon** in August of 2000 posed threats to that country's industry and hence to American computer companies. Dan Briody and Terho Uimonen contributed an article "PC manufacturers await quake impacts," in the Sept. 22, 1999 issue of *Infoworks;* David P. Hamilton and Dean Takahashi provided a similar article, "PC Makers Worry About Memory Chip Shortages," for the Oct. 4, 1999 issue of the *Wall Street Journal;* and Gary McWilliams discussed the impact of the typhoon in an article, also in the *Wall Street Journal,* titled "Shortages of an Intel Microprocessor Create Backlogs, Headaches," published August 23, 2000.

Nearly **as important** to the computer industry as manufacturing and production is the matter of marketing. Initially, the large, established computer companies ignored the possibility of developing the PC because they mistakenly believed that there would be no market for the small, relatively inexpensive computer. **Targeting a market**, anticipating market demand, moving merchandise and other marketing concerns have presented challenges within the entire computer industry, challenges that the various companies have not met consistently because—as was true in the industry's infancy—they have lacked detailed planning and efficient product control. Articles in publications such as *Business Week, The Wall Street Journal, Sales and Marketing Management* and *Brandweek* serve to demonstrate the challenges posed by a fluctuating and often unpredictable market.

**Peter Burrows** contributed an article titled "**The Big Squeeze in the PC Market**" to the September 20, 1999 issue of *Business Week*. Writes Burrows, "When the market for sub—$1,000 personal computers took off a couple of years back, scores of **small companies** saw their chance: With the top brands focused on more profitable machines, they had an open field. Now, it's closing in…. 'As the top brands press down, the guys at the bottom get squeezed to death,' says Chuck Cebuhar, general manager of Sears, Roebuck & Co.$^{TM}$'s home electronics unit."

Burrows notes that "**The big guys** can afford to play and win at the low end because of falling component prices," and he acknowledges some successful strategies of the large computer companies: "PC makers also have cut costs, outsourcing almost all PC production and paring inventory costs with just-in-time deliveries to dealers." **The large companies not only sell PCs for as little as $499, but they offer $400 rebates to customers who agree to sign up with selected Internet service providers**. The result is, "shoppers are using those rebates to buy top brand PCs, not to take home no-names for no money down" (Burrows, 1). Burrows concludes that "[T]he lack of any middle ground makes it next to impossible for entrepreneurs trying to create the next great computer company" (Burrows, 2).

Four journal articles deal directly with the marketing struggles of Compaq$^{TM}$, the computer company within which and for which the POR was designed, and they are useful because they permit the writer to pull together a composite—though certainly incomplete—"picture" of Compaq's marketing maneuvering, successful and otherwise, without venturing into information that would be classified as confidential. "Compaq tries to reboot," an article by Tricia Campbell, appeared in the July 1999 issue of *Sales and Marketing Management*. The title suggests that Compaq has been "down"—and Campbell explains, "[T]oday things aren't going so well for Compaq. In early April the Houston-based company announced disappointing first-quarter revenues of $9.4 billion, about 50 percent below analysts' expectations." Campbell goes on to state "Many analysts believe that Compaq's problems stem from a loss of focus, as it tried to compete with direct-sales juggernauts, like **Dell** while simultaneously utilizing its vast reseller network. Selling PCs directly to customers did slightly reduce Compaq's inventory, but failed to produce the hoped-for efficiency" (Campbell, 1). Campbell asserts that Compaq is attempting to "**re-boot**" by "once again concentrating on its traditional sales channels," but she concludes that "Whether the company will challenge Dell in the direct-sales arena remains to be seen" and warns that "Compaq will need to find a creative way to appease its dealers" (Campbell, 1-2).

Characteristic of the roller-coaster nature of the computer industry, two Year 2000 articles report on favorable market moves by Compaq. Walter S. Mossberg's January 6th article in the *Wall Street Journal,* "Compaq's New Series Has a Quaint Old Look And Slick New Features," opens with the statement that "The first new PC design of the 21st century is a throwback to the 1900s—the early 1900s."

**Mossberg is enthusiastic** about the new computer line's "quaint old look" and about its "user friendly" features—but, even so, he mentions some significant shortcomings: "freeze-ups" which Compaq attributed to preproduction software on Mossberg's test machine; e-mail that doesn't work quite right and doesn't work with America Online, the world's biggest e-mail provider; the fan is a bit noisy; and the online technical-help software has little information on the machine's special features (Mossberg, 1-2). Mossberg's superficially enthusiastic review of the new computer is, thus, a very mixed bag because it is replete with notations about the sort of so-called "minor" imperfections that are a source of irritation and dissatisfaction with consumers. **Ann M. Mack writes** another upbeat article for the September 28th issue of *Brandweek* entitled "Engage links marketing deal with Compaq[TM]," but Mack's optimism has more to do with the benefits that she deduces Engage will realize from the deal than with marketing strides Compaq may be making. **A final article, Todd Wasserman's' "'Customer view' defines Compaq's' branding tack," published in *Brandweek*, October 9, 2000,** is pertinent to this study because it is reporting on ways in which Compaq is handling a number of the issues that are addressed in the **POR**.

**Wasserman** opens his article by quoting **Doug Fox**, svp-marketing and strategy, "Compaq is taking a cautious approach to its latest 'branding campaign, weighing consumer response before it plots long-range expansion."

The careful approach outlined by Fox, looking at business results and fine-tuning the campaign over time, is an approach for which the POR is specifically suited and could prove an effective tool. **It is noted that "Compaq[TM] is focusing the campaign from a customer's point of view**, rather than an inside-out approach of making broad claims."(Wasserman, 1). It is surely relevant that the **POR highlights** consumer response and channels that response both into improving the quality of the product and into directing the marketing of the product. Consumer response—too often in the form of consumer complaints—was a major concern of the POR design team. In fact, the most powerful motivation for designing such a plan was probably the continual flood of consumer calls, messages, letters and reports that crossed the desks of the three individuals who comprised the team.

The **necessity** of recognizing and acknowledging consumer complaints, of processing suggestions or demands for changes and additions, and of underscoring and retaining whatever worked and was well received spurred the team on in their search for ways to insure that these details would be corrected or incorporated in the product at the design level and that consumers' preferences and needs would be efficiently met.

[Compaq$^{TM}$ company policy prohibits examining the consumer feedback to which the POR team had access in their professional capacities. Therefore, it is helpful to look at such feedback as it is expressed or reported in various journals and periodicals.]

**Jared Sandberg** hardly needs to go beyond his rather cumbersome title in his April 25, 2001 article in the *Wall Street Journal:* "**Why Combo Gizmos Don't Cut It**—TV-PCs, Web-Access Phones Show That Whole Can Be Less Than Sum of Its Parts." Periodically, consumer and other companies, fascinated with the promise of "convergence," try to entice consumers by randomly mixing things together and coming up with something hasn't been done before. Sandbert warns that such hybrid devices rarely perform satisfactorily (Sandbert, B1). In "**Testing, testing…1, 2, 3,**" *Network World,* **February 19, 2001, Barry Nance** offers advice about dealing with vendors who give excuses for their product's shortcomings. Michael Munger's "The Computer Industry Is So Predictable," *The Mac Observer: On The Flip Side,* April 11, 2000, claims, "**The industry lacks the ability to produce anything original**" (Munger, 1). He doesn't like the beige towers and the almost identical software titles. He grumbles about the **Mac copycats**, like **eMachines**$^{TM}$. Munger's peeves seem minor, and he is possibly primarily irritated with computer companies suing each other for pirating ideas when they are all so much alike anyway, but such seemingly inconsequential details are important to consumers and require attention.

An ambitious advertising ploy introduced by several computer companies, most of them fly-by-night companies with questionable futures, has been to offer **free PCs to customers who signed up for certain Internet services**.

In an **August 9, 1999 article** in *Time,* **Anita Hamilton** confesses that she found one such offer a "Tempting Deal." She points out the usual drawbacks to such offers: "Companies like Gobi, Intersquid, and ePCdirect require you to pay up to $30 a month for Net access and are rife with hidden fees for basics like a monitor, tech support and one-time 'start-up' charges.

And then there's the nagging fear that these newcomers will vanish into cyber-space long before your three-year contract is up" (Hamilton, 75). Hamilton was finally "tempted" by an offer from FreePC, a 333-MHz Compaq PC with full Internet and e-mail access—in return for filling out a questionnaire, watching ads onscreen and using the computer for 10 hours a month. **Hamilton declares** that she was pleasantly surprised by this set-up, even though ads took up part of her screen and her new PC lacked a 3-D graphics accelerator or top-of-the-line pro-cessor. She points out that it is **hard to get a Free-PC; more than 1 million people applied for the first 10,000** (another case, incidentally, where demand far exceeded expectations and production).

**Two additional articles** are especially relevant to this study in that they approach the computer market from the standpoint of the consumer and detail a number of the problem areas which result, ultimately, in customer dissatisfaction. In a *Wall Street Journal* article, "**Be on Your Guard For These 10 Little Lies As You Shop for a PC**" (January 18, 2001), Walter S. Mossberg begins by stating that he regards the biggest misleading claim made by computer companies to be the notion that higher processor speeds, as measured in megahertz, usually deliver greater actual performance—which he insists just isn't so. Then he goes on to point out misleading claims in ten important areas. Many lower-priced machines don't actually deliver the full 64 or 128 megabytes of **memory** or Ram they claim; lots of machines are described as "**Internet-ready**" but few are any more Internet-capable than any others; standard monitors never deliver the **screen sizes** they tout; many laptop makers state the **weight** of their laptops in an unre-alistic and misleading manner; laptop makers claims about **battery life are almost always overstated**; figures given for **CD-ROM** speed are generally mis-leading; printer makers in claiming **speed in pages per minute** refer to printing at the machines' economy settings, which produce the worst output and aren't commonly used—a fact they do not clarify; much touted "**high speed V.90 modems**" are actually just dial-up phone numbers, and they are quite slow com-pared with today's broadband speeds; companies that offer **On-site Warranties** often force customers to go through an **exhausting and frustrating process** of trying to diagnose the problem themselves before they will consider dispatching a technician; and **Bundled Software** included on the PC often turns out to be spe-cial "light" versions of the retail software, minus some features and often lacking manuals (Mossberg, 1-2). These are areas in which "**duped**" **customers** finally experience disappointment and frustration, and if the customers themselves do not figure out that there are disparities between the quality and capabilities of the actual product and market representations of it, then there are annalists and consumer advocates who will alert them to the fact. In *Have You Got Gremlins*, John C. Dvorak, who provides an Internet computer-help website, points out that the Gremlin automobile is now extinct because it did not deliver what owners had come to expect of an automobile.

He insists that, **like automobile owners**, computer owners have a right to "expect a dependable machine that will deliver a product when it is needed…without having to raise the hood on it every time they get ready to go for a drive" or having to change the engine or upgrade the transmission if they want to attach some essential like a trailer. While Dvorak urges computer users to expect the same quality of product from a computer that they expect from an automobile, he points out that, in contrast to the automobile industry, the base level data and procedures necessary to identify the "**Gremlins**" of the computer world are in "very short supply" (Dvorak, 1).

# The Obvious Need For The Plan
## of Record

By way of concluding this review of the literature pertinent to this book, it may be helpful to use another of **John C. Dvorak's articles**, "The Computer Industry Slowdown," appearing January 3, 2001 in *Net News*. Dvorak begins with the conviction, **"It's time all the computer companies look within their organizations to see exactly what's gone wrong. Why hasn't the typical computer user upgraded to a gigahertz—speed machine**, for example?" Then he proceeds to discuss his "thoughts on the slowdown." Dvorak posits first that, as they once did in the PC industry's infancy, computer companies **need to generate** a "**buzz**" to get people "**jazzed**" about buying machines and continually upgrading. He advocates "**compelling**" **software** and a **buzz-filled atmosphere**. Secondly, he points out that computer companies have stopped advertising heavily, especially in computer magazines, and have come to rely on their ad agencies' "media buyers," people who, he believes, "could care less about computers." Significantly, he suggests that the computer companies need to be "controlling their own fates a little better." Third, **Dvorak says that computer makers seem to be taken in by competitive propaganda and have been hoodwinked into believing such notions as the "thin client" theory and the nonsense about how the PC is dead.**

The implication is that a computer company should be self sufficient enough, and have the tools in place, to deduce what is happening with regard to their own production and sales, allowing them to respond cautiously if at all to external movements and "**To be successful**," Dvorak insists, "the package should empower the individual and allow users to program the application in some customized way' (Dvorak, 1-2). **The software should satisfy the user's** "need for control." Dvorak's fifth and final point is that, as he puts it, "**legacy agony is killing progress**," and he blames this disastrous trend on Microsoft™. He points out that making Windows so reliant on Registry and INI files that applications cannot safely be moved from machine to machine without complete reinstallation is not even good business for Microsoft. He fears that this situation will worsen and "bring down the whole industry" (Dvorak, 3). **Dvorak's assessment that computer companies need to be "controlling their own fates a little better" echoes the convictions of the POR team as they considered the prospect of designing an orderly, foolproof process that would enhance the methods and the results of producing Internet products.**

**The Plan of Record**, which takes the existing two models for product control, the **SPC and TQC**, and expands upon them, is potentially a tool that, in the first place, would enable a computer company to go into manufacturing with at least **99.9% confidence** that the products coming off the assembly line will measure up to design specifications and will be consistent in quality; **furthermore, the POR provides** an orderly means both for ascertaining market conditions and demand and for examining statistically consumer response to various marketing strategies; finally, **the POR facilitates** a continuing and immediate looping back from the end product—and the **feedback** encountered in **Customer Service—into design and manufacturing**, so that improving product quality is automatic and ongoing.

**In other words, the Plan of Record is** the way in which a computer company can "control its own fate a little better." As the historical literature reviewed in this chapter indicates, the personal computer industry in its beginnings was a "run away," out of control; and as the current, industry-related articles strongly suggest, it is still a nervous industry characterized by false starts, miscalculations, set-backs, and failures. **The Plan of Record provides** a process for achieving order and stability within the computer company itself, thus minimizing the company's vulnerability to volatile outside forces.

# Researching, Developing and Implementing The Plan of Record

In the previous overview of the historical evolution of the computer industry and a cursive examination of the nature of the personal computer industry, specifically, and the problems encountered by the numerous companies engaged in manufacturing and marketing PCs, it was demonstrated that, from its inception to the present, that industry has been, paradoxically, both highly competitive and lacking in effective systems for strategic product management and quality control.

Two product management information systems or processes were eventually developed in attempts to bring order and some degree of uniformity to the production and marketing of **PCs** and to **insure product quality—first the (SPC) Statistical Process Control and then the (TQC) Total Quality Control.**

While both systems were successful, at least temporarily, in their goals of improving conditions within the growing and volatile PC industry, they ultimately proved inadequate in the face of rapidly changing technology and the economic upheaval created by an ever-increasing multiplicity of competing companies, large and small, and an expanding but unpredictable market. With the emergence of the Internet and the World Wide Web, computer companies were offered the grand vista of a global market, the potential of which challenged the imagination. But this promising prospect had its down side, as well.

**In terms of product management and quality control**—from design and production all the way through marketing and customer service—most computer companies were not ready to handle a global Internet market (Freed, 1993). In their efforts to compete for their piece of the **"global Internet consumer pie"** many companies—most of them small and enterprising—miscalculated, put themselves at risk, and folded. Even large, well-entrenched companies were jolted by unforeseen demands on manufacture and production and by the giddy slumps and surges of a mammoth, mostly untested market.

**By 1998**, as selections from publications in the previous chapter indicate, an assortment of problems had begun to manifest themselves **throughout the PC**

**industry** in general. Compaq Computer Corporation™, and three Subject Companies was beset by many question's and concerns, coming from customers, computer manufacturers and suppliers of computer products and services. Clearly, for instance, it had become necessary to find ways of improving and gauging build processes.

Just as important, it was essential to devise a system so that customers could have direct feedback into IPC, **BTO** and **CTO build processes** to make a better product and to more adequately meet market demand. Stated simply, manufacturers were compelled to find ways to improve their bottom line.

# Proposing The Plan of Record

This position involves researching and finding solutions to problems such as those mentioned above. Senior Management was approached with the possibility of developing a system for strategic product management and quality control that would incorporate the existing systems, the **SPC** and **TQC**, but that would be comprehensive and exacting enough to meet the needs of **Compaq**™**, and other companies as well**, in their struggles to maintain economic stability in an intensely competitive and nervous industry. This suggestion was approved, and what would eventually become the **POR** was launched.

In many respects, a free hand with regard to how to go about researching and designing the projected system or process was given by management. However, there were certain significant restrictions. There would be no publishing of any kind of "raw data"—information that each company that would be included in the study would consider confidential (logs, meetings, specific target dates, specific systems for storing data, and methods for accessibility, for example).

Furthermore, it was required that the "subject" companies other than Compaq Computer Corporation™ not be identified by name. It was permissible, however, to reveal the categories and results as identified in the study/methodology for these companies (which would be referred to as D, H and I.).

[It should be noted, as has been indicated already, that these restrictions limit the kinds of data and other information that can be used in this book.] **Assured** that the "**go ahead**" and a **firm executive commitment** to the proposal had been given, the next order of business was to create an effective team for pursuing the research, analysis and organizing that would be involved in developing the kind of system that was envisioned—a new process plan of strategic product management information technology for IPCs globally.

The core team consisted of cross-functioning team members and a team leader. These experts in there fields were hand-picked, each having in excess of 20 years of computer program management experience; furthermore, each individual had ten years of work experience with one or more of the top three IPC companies globally. Their experience ranged from component, supplier and product review to customer satisfaction surveys.

The core team would be based in the United States, but as individuals the team members spent a substantial amount of time in each important global region, i.e. Europe, Latin America, Asia and Australia during the research period. At the time when the team was scheduled to begin researching the project (**December of 1999**), human resources were limited at best; nevertheless, once the core group of three was assembled, consideration was given to broadening the team. However, the strain on human resources throughout the company and, probably more significantly, security and confidentiality requirements seemed to dictate a small, easily mobile and personally dedicated team—so after due consideration the idea of adding members to the original core team was dismissed. What was decided was that as the core team implemented the new strategic product management methodology, the IPC companies and supplier organizations would become part of the team as a whole, an arrangement, which promised to be, and indeed was, extremely effective with communications. **Setting Goals**, **Organizing Research** and **Identifying Resources** with the core team was in place, the next concern was to arrive at a name for the system that the team was committed to researching and developing; for in an endeavor such as the one the team was tackling, the name helps to clarify, identify and limit the nature of the project and, thus, helps to focus the energies of those who are striving toward its realization.

**A good name** can also stir the imagination, generate enthusiasm, and suggest a measure of attainment beyond the ordinary. After some serious discussion, the name POR, Plan Of Record (PORI, Plan-of-Record Index and CSI, Customer Service Index) was chosen on the basis of clear definitions of the words.

"**Plan**" is defined as a foundation and a method for achieving. For the three team members, thinking in terms of providing a foundation and searching for and developing a method helped to set forth precisely what the team expected to be doing, and achieving or achievement was what it was hoped would be the end results of those efforts.

**The word "Record"** has multiple meanings, two of which seemed to have direct bearing the project. The word "Record" is defined, first, as something that recalls or relates past events, and it was that this definition applied well to the fact that the team would incorporate globally practiced systems—SPC and TQC—as the more ambitious "Plan" was devised. "Record" is also defined as relating to, or being one that is extraordinary among or surpasses others of its kind. It was the aim of the Core Team that the "Plan" being developed would surpass existing systems and that in doing so, it would enable Compaq and other companies to be extraordinary among or surpass others of their kind. With the project named to team members' mutual satisfaction, simple short and long term goals toward which endeavors could be focused. The **short-term goals** were to **identify** the existing product management process information technology, to identify suppliers and manufacturers of IPCs that would most benefit from the projected research, and to look for key areas for testing the methodology processes, product quality, market share, manufacture, service, training, program review and customer impact in terms of **CTO** and **BTO** of **IPCs**. The team's long-term goal was set to identify financial-impact on IPC manufacturers and suppliers.

**In addition to setting goals**, team members arrived at a time frame for developing the system that was envisioned. Various pressures both within the company and without made it mandatory that the team moves toward workable solutions as rapidly as possible. Six months would have been an ideal time for working on and completing the project; however, it was understood that there could be interruptions and complications, so an attempt was made to stay within a realistic and flexible time-frame, allowing six months to a year for completing and perfecting the POR.

**Meetings and possible itineraries** were scheduled for the first six months of proposed research and study. As stated, logs, meetings, specific target dates and other such information are regarded as confidential, so it is impossible to offer further details in that regard. **Deciding upon and making arrangements** for the resources that research, observation and perhaps even experimentation would require was another step in the preparatory phase of the team's work on the project. Members identified and created a Ready Reference Library to keep the core team grounded. This Library consisted of the following book references: Marketing Planning & Strategy (1993) by Subbash C. Jain; Organizational Behavior Concepts, Controversies and Applications (1979–1991) by Stephen P. Robbins; Managerial Economics Text, Problems and Short Cases (1959–1991) by K. K. Seo; The Managerial Decision Making Process (1995) by E. Frank Harrison; Psychology and Work Today (1973–1990) by Duane P. Schultz and Sydney Ellen Schultz; Business Research Methods (1991) by William G. Zikmund and Marketing Management Analysis Planning, Implementation & Control (1967–1991) by Philip Kotler.

**Members were at liberty to bring** to the attention of the core team other books, pamphlets, instruction guides and documents that seemed likely to prove necessary and useful, and some of these materials—often items that were classified and confidential—were added to the basic library. The Core Team reviewed the possible needs with regard to additional resources.

**It was fortunate** that within Compaq$^{TM}$—and within the subject companies that would eventually be identified as **D, H and I** as well—**a structure already existed** which, for the most part, provided the supporting human and systems resources that our work would require. The Core Team was, after all, starting with the **SPC** (Statistical Process Control) and **TQC** (Total Quality Control), which had been in place and carefully implemented for several years. Compaq and the subject companies, once they were selected, would each be part of the new methodology, making the existing resources immediately available for expanding the programs currently in use to the more comprehensive and exacting demands of the POR. **The specific resources** that were required for this methodology will be identified in connection with the **Dependent and Independent Variables** later in this chapter. There were, of course, minor challenges that arose as the Core Team widened its research and development to include companies in other parts of the world. For instance, team members encountered language differences and a need for effective translators, but were able to resolve this problem with employees in each country who spoke English fluently.

**With goals in mind and resources in place** and duly noted, the first step in research and development was to identify all of the categories within the industry, from manufacturing through marketing, that had to be examined and monitored in terms of product management and quality control. In order to come up with these complex variables, the team used the existing information from **SPC** and **TQC** as a starting point and broadened the spectrum gradually as additional and more pertinent information was accumulated, investigating **IS0900X$^{TM}$** and **Six Sigma$^{TM}$**—statistical process control as well. It was then necessary to identify these categories in each of the subject companies; as a matter of fact, the selection of subject companies **D, H and I** was an end result of **identifying the requisite categories** in the numerous companies that are vendors and suppliers for Compaq Computer Corporation$^{TM}$ and determining the extent to which each was functioning effectively in terms of a given category. **Subject companies D, H and I** were chosen on the basis of these considerations: (1) they have the highest volume capacity to build a product worldwide; **Six Sigma** was not found to be a world-wide acceptable process during this time, as it was to expensive and human resource intensive, and not cost justified, **however** it did utilize statistical process controls **SPC$^{TM}$** and customer methods that were beneficial and found in **TQC$^{TM}$**. (2) They have the highest quality of whatever product is being shipped; (3) of all the companies examined, they worked best in the areas of Warranty and Customer Satisfaction and Serviceability. Before team members went "**on the**

**road**" to meet with the companies that would participate in the new methodology.

**It was essential** to demonstrate to team members' own satisfaction—and certainly to the satisfaction of Senior Management—that the new methodology worked. For this purpose the team made use of an already existing resource, Building 5P. This is a building that is set up to provide an accurate environment, on a small scale, for each of the major phases of the computer industry—design, manufacture and production, marketing, and consumer response and service. Companies in anticipating of a new and future technology, Senior Management would approve a pilot build in limited quantity (usually about 50) and the product is taken through the industry process from beginning to end. Within Building 5P a mini-manufacturing plant is already set up, and assemblers, technicians, engineers, management staff and analysis's are already on hand. With the help of these special employees, the Core Team took a test product through the manufacturing process, following POR guidelines, and used the PORI (Plan of Record Index) to verify that the manufacturing was completed. The PORI-verified products were then taken to another room in Building 5P, aptly called "Human Factors." **Here customers examine and use the product and provide invaluable feedback.**

[Needless to say, everything that happens in the Human Factors Room is highly confidential; customers sign a nondisclosure agreement, and the details of their feedback are classified. The members of the Core Team were able to question customers, using POR categories, and that feedback was written down and incorporated in the POR.]

When the results of the experimental process in Building 5P were determined to be positive—in other words, using the **POR and the PORI** was demonstrated to be an **improvement over the SPC and TQC**—team members were ready to "hit the road" with the new methodology. Not only were team members able to approach the three subject companies with confidence in the effectiveness of the POR and the PORI, but consumer feedback **CSI** from the "Human Factors" phase of the trial run had provided the most current information available to date on design, manufacture and marketing. The team had already established that the three subject companies, **D, H and I**, had attained a level of quality and utilized product processes that were closely in line with what it was proposed would be tested with the PORI; now the team knew—at least with much greater accuracy than had been possible before—which items in the POR categories to look for when a new product was to be produced. Either singly or together, the three coordinators met with each of the subject companies, spending extended periods of time in their country and visiting with the people employed in each company. The team's purpose was to understand as well as was possible their thought patterns, their values, and their work ethic. **But it was crucial** to understand what their manufacturing processes were, as well, and that required much more than talk. The Core Team wanted to see real documents, reports that could be verified and compared with the **POR**. Thus, the team reviewed company documents such as quality reports, manufacturing data, and yield reports (how many units could they actually build?). When all of this information was collected and sorted, the next move was to measure or test it using the **PORI/CSI** (Plan of Record Index, Customer Satisfaction Index). **Setting Up Categories for Testing**.

**Granted, such testing presented challenges**. Many of the categories the team has come up with in the POR/PORI/CSI are new in the field, based on the most current information available. Therefore, the team combined the historical systems, **SPC** and **TQC**, with the most current information available to date. The following chart indicates the "**Categories to Test**" from the Plan of Record Index—which, it will be noted, calls for **a mathematical measurement in each category listed**. The design of the experiment is presented in the chart below, with examples of the rating processes referenced within the procedure.

# Plan of Record Performance Index (PORI)

Categories to Test

Plan of Record

| Readiness | Measured by: Product | Goals: | 19XX | 2XXX |
|---|---|---|---|---|
| 1. Processes | Short Delivery Cycle % | | | |
| 2. Product Quality | Incoming Material % | | | |
| 3. Market Share | Competitor % | | | |
| 4. Manufacture | Readiness % | | | |
| 5. Services | Readiness % | | | |
| 6. Training | Asset Utilization % | | | |
| 7. Program Review | Flex for Mix Changes % | | | |
| 8. Customer Impact | CST | | | |

With the Categories to Test clearly established, it became possible to proceed with the study or experiment that the Core Team had determined would be its primary task. The Design of that experiment is as follows:

## DESIGN OF EXPERIMENT

## Subjects

Four leading Internet personal computer product producers have been selected for this study. Each is measured by the same criteria. These **companies are identified** as companies **Compaq, D, H and I**. The company name is confidential for

D, H and I. [The "raw data" for companies Compaq, D, H and I are confidential, but are included in results, assumptions and generalizations that are provided within this book.]

# Procedure

The procedure for the rating guidelines is outlined in Figure 1. Design of Experiment. Subject companies were surveyed on eight categories: Processes, Components, Market MRD, Manufacture, Services, Training, Program Review and Customer Impact (CSI). Subjects were surveyed for the Plan of Record Performance Index in the areas of Processes, Components, Market, Manufacture, Services, Training, Program Review and Customer Impact (CSI).

# Survey Scores

Survey scores are identified within the study as a percentage (0-100%) of the Plan of Record Performance Index Plan. The information planning system rating is as follows:

# Figure 1. Design of Experiment

Subjects will be tested according to the Plan of Record (PORI) Index Survey Scale, Production Impact, and the Customer Satisfaction Table. Test scores are identified by the Auditor as a percentage (0%-100%) of meeting the Plan of Record (POR) production rating. The system rating is as follows:

# Rating Guidelines

| Rating | Definition |
|--------|------------|
| NA | Not Applicable—Indicate available points = 0 |
| 1. | The item/procedure is NOT included in the Product plan. |
| 2. | The item/procedure is included in the Product plans and is generally acceptable; However, the level of planning or execution still requires improvement. |

| Rating | Definition |
|---|---|
| 3. | The item/procedure is included in the Product plan. Planning and execution meet requirements. |
| 4. | The item/procedure is included in the Product plan. Planning and execution is Thorough and outstanding. |

A Subsystem and Element scoring are utilized and focus in on the Plan of Record Performance Index and have been designated as Subsystem and Elements within the survey information planning system. The Element Rating equals the total scored points, divided by the total available points. The Subsystem Rating equals the Element score (%) X Weight. The Survey Rating equals the Subsystem one through eight totals. Thus, 0-20 (%) = Unacceptable; 21-40 (%) = Significant Deficiency; 41-78 (%) = Improvement Needed; 79-98 (%) = **Satisfactory**; 99-100 (%) = Outstanding Plan of Record Performance.

# Identifying Independent and Dependent Variables

The following Independent Variables are matched to their Dependent Variables or by an alphabetical reference, **A** through **W**. For example, **Dependent Variable**, *Plan of Record Checklist*, has an **Independent Variable** of the letter A being Pre-survey.

| Dependent Variables | Independent Variables |
|---|---|
| Plan of Record Survey Checklist | A |
| Executive Summary | B |
| Global Product Deployment | C |
| System Volume expectations and transition plan | D |
| CTO and BTO business components | E |
| Marketing Requirements Document (MRD) | F |
| Business components | G |
| Quality Training requirements | H |
| Customer satisfaction impact system | I |
| Quality Goals and Deployment System | J |
| New Features | K |

| Dependent Variables | Independent Variables |
|---|:---:|
| Services Schedules | <u>L</u> |
| Program risks | <u>M</u> |
| Projected volumes | <u>N</u> |
| Factory Equipment Tools defined and ordered | <u>O</u> |
| Bill of Materials (BOM) structured | <u>P</u> |
| Manufacturing Process Flow System for PCA | <u>Q</u> |
| CPU, Manufacturing Test Strategy | <u>R</u> |
| Testing and Diagnosis System | <u>S</u> |
| Ramp Plan System | <u>T</u> |
| Material Requirements System Board | <u>U</u> |
| Final Acceptance and Quality Feedback System | <u>V</u> |
| Calibrate and Gage Repeatability and Reproducibility | <u>W</u> |

**The Independent Variables** signified by upper case letters in the column at right in the table above will be discussed as well as the Dependent Variables. A detailed examination of the Independent Variables serves both to clarify the industry needs, which the Plan of Record (POR, PORI and CSI) was designed to meet and to demonstrate the implementation of the plan.

In terms of this information, it is sufficient to point out that the Rating System, or set of tools for measurement, outlined above allows for a simple, direct and practical application.

A **review of Independent and Dependent Variables** gives percentage numbers for each major industry category (and these remain stable and consistent from one company to the next). It is thus possible to have an exact measurement of the effectiveness of a company's production in each category.

[For the purpose of the Core Team's study during the experimental-initiatory stage of developing the POR, those measurements could then be compared to performance in each category after the POR was in place—and it was possible to determine not only whether the plan had resulted in improvement but the degree of such improvement.]

**SPC, TQC and POR Flow Charts** by way of conclusion and recapitulation, the Flow Charts which the Core Team followed as they developed the Plan of Record may be helpful. **In the beginning, as the Team contemplated** what must be done, it was necessary to follow the same line of progression in our thinking that the PC industry had followed in its brief and tumultuous history. infancy when components were brought together, partly through guess-work and partly through inspiration, and assembled in some hobbyist's garage—with no certainty what the final product would look like or whether it would work in the way intended.

Team members had to imagine and articulate for themselves the profound changes that had to occur in order for this haphazard process to evolve into an assembly line that could turn out even a fairly large quantity of units that were efficient—and appealing—in design and at least somewhat consistent in performance.

**During this growing phase** of the industry's history, quality expectations were set, but were still specific to the business market. **Each generation** of producing computer products was separate and distinct and did not have a sense of connection; rather each computer product component operated on its own.

Thus, the **SPC emerged** as the most effective product management information process tool for regulating the production of computer products—though it was hardly an adequate tool for regulating production globally because of differences in market requirements. **The Flow Chart spread begins with SPC next page:**

$$\boxed{SPC}$$

(STATISTICAL PROCESS CONTROL)

| SUPPLIER |
| START—Ensure material improvement processes |

| OEM |
| 2nd—Measurement of Systems and unit evaluation |

| CUSTOMER |
| FINISH—Meet product expectation |

Amsden, Robert T., Butler, Howard E., and Amsden, David M. 1980. SPC Simplified. White Plains, NY: UNIPUB/Kraus International Publications. P. 105. It will be noted that the SPC consists of three components, Supplier, OEM (Original Equipment Manufacturer) and Customer. Each component has a specific expectation.

The expectation is to ensure material improvement processes. These processes are accomplished, first, by identifying the need for and making necessary changes to the methodology involved in assembling each piece part, and, second, by determining what its relevant piece part cost is to the next step in this process—which is the OEM.

The **OEM** (Original Equipment Manufacturer) has an expectation that encompasses the measurement of systems. **This means** that the OEM examines what the test requirements and design expectations of the product are and evaluates product "**fall-out**" (in manufacturing—the units that do not pass the test). The Customer component has an expectation that the computer product manufacturer will meet "Customer product standards." **These standards** were identified by general market (Customer) research that included Basic Form and Fit and Functionality of the product line. **In the early 1980s,** the SPC model was used for many reasons, one of which was as the information product management technology to produce computer products for business-specific application markets; gradually it came to be utilized as a consumer computer product management market tool as well. Because SPC became increasingly inadequate in terms of complex industry demand, **TQC** was developed to augment it. As the flow chart gradually evolves from **SPC to TQC**, it becomes clear that "**quality**" is intensified with SPC to **create TQC**.

$$\boxed{\quad \text{TQC} \quad}$$

(TOTAL QUALITY COMMITMENT)

| SUPPLIER |
|---|
| START—Ensure material improvement processes |

| |
|---|
| 2nd—SUPPLIER, Also ship material JIT (Just-In-Time) for manufacturing |

| OEM |
|---|
| 3rd—Measurement of Systems and unit evaluation |

| CUSTOMER |
|---|
| FINISH—Meet product expectation, include customer surveys |

Shonberger, Richard. 1991. World class manufacturing casebook: Implementing JIT and TQC. New York: Free Press.

The **key** items **between SPC and TQC** involve quality enhancement, utilizing JIT (Just-in-Time) manufacturing to address piece part cost-to-build and deliver information as well as general customer service, **TQC became** a very effective computer product management information process tool in the early to the late **1990s**. The **turning point** for TQC came when the global market changed and computer products became "Internet computer products" for consumers as well as businesses worldwide. **The SPC and TQC models no longer meet the needs of the new market demand by them self's, However**, SPC and TQC models did establish a strong foundation from which to move forward into what is now called **POR** (Plan of Record) and its components (**PORI/CSI**). **POR combines** both of the historical methods, SPC and TQC, to introduce the newest and most valuable model/method, a process plan of strategic product management information control being practiced globally. Following page is the Flow Chart spread for the **Plan of Record (POR):**

## POR

### (PLAN OF RECORD, PORI, CSI)

---

START—Strategic Product Planning, key activities, key deliverables and controls

---

$2^{nd}$—Costs—Identify product development expenses—people

---

$3^{rd}$—Product definition—Identify product functionality, market requirements, quality goals and metrics per product unit, cost goals and warranty targets

---

$4^{th}$—Identify Suppliers—True Partnerships, expectations, business framework, Supplier recognition, processes

---

$5^{th}$—Create Core Team—Schedule, specifies the scheduling for all program deliverables (i.e., from ALL functional organizations)

---

$6^{th}$—Product development—POR approved by Core Team and Division

---

$7^{th}$—Design and System Integration—Create prototype plans and target and set pilot build plans

---

$8^{th}$—Implement pilot build—Product validation, and manufacturing verification build

---

$9^{th}$—Implement product validation pilot—Build sufficient Systems, test reports, per program POR

10th—Implement manufacturing verification—Build revenuable Systems, fulfill internal unit requests per program POR

11th—Implement production Ramp—Build Service spare parts, build product options, per program POR

12th—Implement PORI plan—Plan of Record Index, this measures and evaluates company and market goals

FINISH—Customer satisfaction initiative, establish common language focus on the customer, feedback and impact new products Strategic planning for next POR

**The POR (Plan of Record)** has an expectation of meeting each new Internet computer product market requirement globally through incorporating the strengths of **SPC and TQC** into its system, expanding upon and enhancing those aspects of these systems that are already historically in place and being utilized world-wide, and then extending the process of strategic product management information control by introducing features that apply to and are effectively responsive to the demands of PC production and marketing on a worldwide or global dimension. **An examination** of the Flow Charts in the POR spread should reveal, for instance, that not only does the POR address the areas of **Supplier**, **OEM** and **Customer**, as did the SPC, but it provides tools or guidelines for **eliminating the elements of guess-work, chance** and **accident in those basic areas.** **What is unique** from **SPC and TQC** is the fact that the **POR** is thorough in its application from strategic product planning through the spectrum of industry processes to effective distribution and marketing. **This is because** the **PORI** (Plan of Record Index) can be utilized to identify company and market goals world-wide, including **CSI** Service and Warranty expectations—and, what especially distinguishes it from previously used systems, **provides feedback from the customer** into the **NEW** up-coming computer product designs that are specific to each region around the world. **The significance** of this last feature can hardly be exaggerated. With SPC and TQC *the approach may be explained as linear,* with no direct connection between planning and design at one end of the industry process and customer response and demand at the other. **When computer com-**

**panies** took on a worldwide or global market, the distance (not so much in miles as in time lapse and adequate means or agency) quickly increased to the point that contact between the two, planning and design and the customers they were attempting to satisfy, was insufficient, and disastrous mismanagement resulted.

**The POR, augmented by the PORI, CSI may be explained as circular**, because it provides for a *looping back* from customer/consumer to planning and design that is direct, automatic, immediate and ongoing—thus insuring that improvement of quality and response to customer demands are integrated into each phase of design, production and marketing.

# Implementing The Plan of Record

To the extent that policies of confidentiality permit, the step by step development of the Plan of Record from the point at which the idea for such a procedure was presented to Senior Management, through the appointment of a Strategic Core Team, and then through some portion of that team's research and experimentation which would result in devising **the Plan of Record (POR) the Plan of Record Index (PORI) and CSI** has been examined.

**It should be fairly obvious** that the very nature of that research and experimentation poses a problem in making any **real distinction** between devising or creating the POR and its implementation: the team devised as it implemented and implemented as it devised. For that reason, among others, the work of the Core Team can be considered empirical research. In the two major divisions of this information, a rather arbitrary and artificial division is made: the early stages of the team's work on the POR are handled under the heading "**Researching and Developing the POR,**" in the second heading is handled as reference is made to "**implementing the plan,**" but it should be understood that the creating and developing process continued with implementation.

# Defining Independent and Dependent Variables

**Clarification** with regard to the difference between Independent and Dependent Variables is also necessary in approaching this present chapter. Once again it is necessary to call attention to certain unique aspects of the personal computer industry, as well as to that industry's equally unique beginnings.

**Two factors to examine** are PC production and marketing: first, the PC is a product that is assembled from components that are acquired from a variety of suppliers; and second, a PC has no one specific function that it is supposed to perform. Historically, these factors have always resulted in unexpected complications within the industry. For instance, a problem with even one supplier of a particular component can seriously limit or halt production, and an unforeseen crisis will exist. In connection with the function factor, customers may envision a function for a computer with certain features—a function not anticipated at the design level and hence not taken into account at the level of production—and a company may find itself trying to cope with consumer demand greater than it can meet.

**Or** the reverse may occur: Design may expect that a segment of the market will respond favorably to a proposed function of a given PC and discover belatedly that there is no customer appeal. As has been previously explained, from it's beginning the PC industry wrestled with chance and accident. **Early PC "nuts"** acquired components as imagination, inspiration and logic directed, assembled them on benches in their garages—and sometimes they worked and sometimes they did not. Sometimes units thus assembled could be duplicated, sometimes produced in quantities large enough to satisfy a growing market—but sometimes such ventures failed.

**It was crucial**, when systems such as **SPC and TQC** were developed, **to single out** industry categories that were stable and could be counted on because the information necessary for operation in those areas was available. Industry categories where the necessary information is available are designated as Independent Variables. **The terms Dependent Variable or Variables** is used to designate industry categories in which information is not readily available. These are, needless to say, the areas in which chance, accident, guesswork, speculation and error hold sway, often to the detriment of the computer company, and these are the areas that a system like the POR is designed to address.

Determining these industry categories, the Independent and the Dependent Variables, was a task that the Core Team tackled even in preliminary research and a task that remained ongoing as study revealed more about the strengths and shortcomings of procedures already in place and those that were being introduced.

**As Figure 1**. Design of Experiment indicates, it was possible to distinguish which Dependent Variable impacts a given Independent Variable. In the above-mentioned Figure 1. The Independent Variables are designated by capital letters to indicate this relationship.

For the purposes of this chapter, however, it seems more meaningful to discuss the implementation of the Independent Variables as they occur within the phases of the industry process—planning and design, manufacturing and production, marketing and customer service—rather than in alphabetical order. The premise upon which the POR (Plan of Record) was developed is that the approach it embodies makes it possible to obtain the kind of information at every stage in the industry process that would eliminate chance and accident and insure quality and marketability in the end product. In this chapter, the Independent Variables will retain their capital letter designations but will be explained in terms of the industry phase to which they relate.

# Planning and Design: Implementing Dependent Variables

At the Planning and Design level, the following Independent Variables apply: A, B, C, F, G, K, and W. Independent Variable A is a Pre-Survey that is a part of the planning the Dependent Variable, the Plan of Record Survey Checklist.

**As has already been explained**, the Plan of Record is unique in that it makes the production and marketing of personal computers and Internet products a circular as opposed to a linear process, so that there is immediate feedback from customers at the end of the industry process back to planning and design at the beginning.

**The tool that facilitates this feedback** is the Dependent Variable, the Plan of Record Survey Checklist. Because this Checklist is in place, the Pre-Survey (Independent Variable A) would indicate "Information Available"—that is, members of the staff in Planning and Design would have specific information about glitches, shortcomings, customer complaints, and customer preferences and suggestions which they can incorporate at the design or re-design level.

Independent Variable B is the Product Summary and impacts the Dependent Variable, the Executive Summary.

# Executive Summary

**Under systems previous to the POR**, the traditional Executive Summary was often generic and imprecise; but with the information made available under Independent Variable A, the product summary can be exact with regard to industry expectations.

For the product introduced by the Core Team in our original implementation, the Product Summary read as follows:

(a) **This new IPC Product Family or code name product will** be designed and marketed globally with the goal of dominating each key price point from $999 to $1,799.

Several system boards will be utilized to effectively cover this product's price points for BTO and CTO Internet product configurations.

(b) **The design of the boards will** allow for a high degree of leverage with graphics and audio solutions among mainstream and performance platforms.

The same graphics family will be used for all boards with a discreet project name, and the same PCI audio solution will be utilized on all non-integrated chipsets.

(c) **The company will introduce** two new industry standard ATX and UATX chassis for Quarter One products. All new industrial designs will be developed around the new chassis designs. Priorities for the second quarter program are profitable products at key retail price points, quality product, time to market, and product feature set.

(d) **The profit goal** for the program is to achieve at least 16% overall life cycle gross margin (monitor included).

The **company customer satisfaction goals** will be met or exceeded. Significant reduction of product returns and service and support calls will be realized through the proper design and implementation of product features. Begin with an initial MVB date of 01/15/XX, and ramp of 03/18/XX.

**Independent Variable C**, Localization, impacts the Dependent Variable, Global Product Deployment.

Prior to the emergence of the Internet, and with it a worldwide market, only passing attention was given to how well a product would be likely to function within a variety of specific environments.

**A product was assembled**, and it functioned as well as it could wherever it might wind up being put into use. **This meant** that products went to market within a broad spectrum of chance with regard to how completely and efficiently they would function for consumers, given each consumer's particular circumstances—and that spectrum of chance existed even when the market did not extend much beyond North America.

But when the Internet opened up a worldwide market, it became absolutely essential to identify the requirements of each world market and to make modifications at each stage of the industry process in order to accommodate those special needs.

**Language requirements** were obvious considerations. Simple but very fundamental inconsistencies like wiring and voltage, for instance—115 in North America, 220 in Europe—were matters that had to be taken into account at the design and production levels in order to realistically expect that a product would be marketable in any given area. Thus, a definite list of projected markets was essential at the beginning of the industry process. **For Independent Variable C**, **Localization**, the research for the product that is the subject of our initial POR implementation identified the following global marketing Locations and they are: North America (NA), APD (Asia), CKK (Japan). EMEA (Europe), and LA (Latin America), APD—Korea, South Chinese, Taiwan—Chinese, CKK—Japan, EMEA, Germany, France, Denmark, Italy, Norway, Portugal, Spain, Sweden, United Kingdom, Latin America English, Brazil builds with Network Integrated Cards. APD English countries include: Hong Kong, India, Indonesia, Malaysia, Philippines, Vietnam, Thailand, and Singapore. Latin America, Spanish countries include (Mexico, Guatemala, El Salvador, Costa Rica, Nicaragua, Honduras, Panama, Argentina, Uruguay, Paraguay, Bolivia, Peru, Ecuador, Venezuela and Columbia).

**Independent Variables F and G** both involve materials and information that are company confidential.

**Independent Variable F**, the *Marketing Requirements Guide*, is directly related to the Dependent Variable, Marketing Requirements Document (MRD). Among the items included in the Guide are Marketing Name, Date, Version (X.I), Legal Statement and the Internet Personal Computer Product (PCP).

*[It is noted that the company will not be liable for technical or editorial errors or omissions contained within the Guide nor for incidental or consequential damages*

*resulting from the furnishings, performance, or use of the material contained in it. Because the product names mentioned in the Guide may be trademarks and/or registered trademarks of their respective companies, the Guide, as has been stated, is considered company confidential—so that the foregoing brief suggestion of its content is all that can be offered.*] **Independent Variable G** impacts on the Dependent Variable, which has to do with Business Components. In this area, the POR suggests strategies whereby members of the staff at the planning-design level can obtain fundamental knowledge of the tools and techniques available and how they link to the quality measures in that department and company business plan, in order that they can arrive at and communicate clear expectations with regard to how the tools/techniques are to be used and establish standards or measures for that use.

**Independent Variable G** also involves sensitive information, which will not be present in detail. During the initial development and implementation of the POR (Plan of Record) that development and implementation was, along with the product used in implementing the Plan, a New Feature—which is the Dependent Variable impacted by **Independent Variable K.** Prior to entering the design phase in the industry process, it was necessary that the POR be approved before adding the new product used in its implementation to the forecast roadmap (which is phase independent). Toward this end, **the POR (Plan of Record) was identified thus "The POR (Plan of Record) is an information tool designed to define the requirements for each new product development.** It will provide **a product positioning statement**, the product description and specification, cost and pricing targets, schedule milestones with regard to product introduction, product deployment, volume expectations and transition plans. The Plan of Record (POR) will **be completed and signed off with detailed PCA** and CPU level product functional definition, new features, procurement plans (OEM/in house), schedules, program risks, and projected volumes.

A complete **product definition** is provided for project planning, resources loading, and *risk analysis*. Details on the Plan of Record (POR) allow corporate manufacturing and operations to resource allocation and loading guidelines, determine and set first-pass unit failure goals, generate test strategy and requirements, predict test times and unique factory test-and-build requirements, recommend deployment plans, perform risk analysis, analyze long range plans and capacity analyses, and perform high level supplier positioning.

The **MRD** (Marketing Requirements Document) a sub-set of POR is available. To facilitate **project planning**, resources loading, and risk analysis—as indicated above—the following product definition was provided for the product that was introduced in the Core Team's initial implementation of the POR (Plan of Record): The **Chassis** that will be utilized are Industrial Standard UATX and ATX.

**UATX Chassis**:

> Boards supported: ATX, Slots: 4-3/4" length or ½ length
> Accessible Drive Bays: 2-(5.25 half-height drive)
> Two—(3.50" drives FDD/Zip/LS120)
> Internal Drive Bays: 1-(5.25" or 3.50" HDD)
> Power Supply: ATX or SFX (75-145 Watts)
> ATX Chassis, Boards supported: ATX or RATX Slots:
> Seven-Full length or ¾" length
> Accessible Drive Bays: 3 (5.25" half-height drive)
> Two (3.50" drives FDD/Zip/LS12O)
> Internal Drive Bay:
> One (5.25" or 3.50" HDD)
> Power Supply: ATX (145-200 Watts)
> I/O specifications (same for either chassis)
> Back I/O Keyboard:
> Mouse USB (2 ports):
> Audio (mic/line-in/line-out)
> XVGA:
> Serial port
> Parallel port:
> Flat panel 1394: (mfg. Option on ATX chassis Only)
> Front I/O.
> USB: (2 ports)
> Game port 1394: (mfg. Option on ATX chassis Only)

The **product name family** of products will be shipped with Windows 98 (WinXX—BTO; WinXX/WinNT—CTO) and be compatible with all Windows applications.

The **drivers** for all applicable company OEM printers will be pre-installed.

**Blue-lining** and **easy access** buttons on the keyboard will work with monitor controls. Fax and video phone software will be pre-installed.

*Third party software* will be Windows XX compatible. Systems will also operate running Windows NT, Other.

***Motherboards.*** ATX Light and ATX Express.

The ATX motherboard is the XXX.

**Light motherboard**. (Motherboards with integrated audio will be foot printed with discreet audio components to mitigate legacy issues (no audio in real mode DOS, or some DOS-box applications) with the integrated audio solutions.

**The maximum** (default-XMB) accessible system memory = total, memory = XXXMB Intel and National; Cyrix Socket XXX processors will be qualified and supported. *Storage Devices*. These devices are DVD, CD-ROM, HDD, Zip Drive, and LS-120 Drive.

*Modem with Home Networking*. Systems will ship with the appropriate modem and Home Networking (HN) configuration on PCI cards. PCI cards currently under evaluation are: V.9X & HN & Base T (NA only), V.90 (Europe and Asia), UDSL and ADSL (NA only), V.90 Combo (NA only BTO-CTO), HN and 10/100 NIC Combo (NA only BTO-CTO).

*Keyboard*. Internet Keyboard with programmable access functions.

*Mouse*. Internet/Scroll mouse.

*Power Management*. Power Management will operate across all platforms. When the unit is power cycled (loss of AC power or toggling the rear power switch from off to on) the unit will boot into Windows (regardless of the power state the computer was in before being power cycled). The unit will enter the sleep mode through three conditions. The sleep-button is pressed while the unit is on. The unit, times out after a thirty-minute period of inactivity. The user selects Start, Shut Down; Shut Down the computer from the toolbar. When the unit is in the sleep mode, pressing the sleep button will restore the unit.

*Industrial Design*. During this product cycle POR evaluation, all ATX designs will be driven into mainstream space where UATX form factors had existed previously. "A component of the success of this study will be to drive the cost of the ATX form factor down to UATX levels. A test of this study will be to highlight core features such as more expandability, accessible front I/O, and Zip (when featured) without the need for more than one feature label. "A futuristic finish (or some way of projecting a futuristic image) will be investigated to take advantage of millennium marketing efforts.

*Software Specifications*. The product name or family of products will be shipped with Win XX (WinME—BTOl; Win/WinNT, Other—CTO) and be compatible with all Windows applications.

*The drivers*. for all applicable company OEM printers will be pre-installed. Blue-lining and easy access buttons on the keyboard will work with monitor controls.

*Fax and video phone software*. will be pre-installed.

**Third party software** will be Windows 29XX compatible. Systems will also operate running Windows NT, Other.

**The foregoing is an example** of a Product Definition, presented as implementation of the POR (Plan of Record) in addressing **Independent Variable K.**

**At the Planning and Design level**, a thorough and exact definition of what the product is expected to be at the completion of the industry process minimizes the elements of guesswork and trial and error.

**Independent Variable W**, Test and Root Cause, which impacts the Dependent Variable, Calibration and Gauging of Repeatability and Reproducibility, would seem to fall at the conclusion of the industry process, or in any case, at the end of pre-build manufacturing—as indeed it does. [But it should be kept in mind that the POR requires an immediate looping back from test results and other feedback that respond to the "finished product" to Planning and Design, at the beginning of the industry process.]

**Thus, Independent Variable K is addressed**, in part, through a thorough and exact definition of the product to be designed and produced; and **Independent Variable W**, which resolves issues involving repeatability and reproducibility as evidenced and measured in assembly, manufacturing and production, loops back full circle—with the result that it is possible to examine the extent to which the original product definition was realized and to modify the inconsistencies or to halt production if the inconsistencies cannot be remedied. In connection with **Independent Variable W** it should be noted that an issue is considered understood if it is accepted by an expert in the field of the problem. **An expert includes**, but is not limited to the areas of design, reliability, agency, product engineering, test engineering, diagnostic engineering, and manufacturing. An issue is considered closed if its resolution has been agreed upon and the implementation of that resolution has begun and will be in place prior to the manufacturing verification build.

**An issue can be considered closed** if an expert decides that the correct response is to take no corrective action. This might arise when the resolution is too costly for the benefit it yields.

# Manufacture and Production: Implementing The Dependent Variables

It may be useful at the outset to note that the Independent Variables involved in the Manufacture-Production phase of the industry process have to do, for the most part, Specifically, with pre-build manufacture and small manufacture. **It is true that from a practical, hands-on standpoint**, the kind of scrutiny and detailed analysis demanded by the POR can occur more realistically and more effectively within the bounds of a small-scale operation. However, the reasoning behind implementing a carefully monitored pre-build and small-scale manufacture of a product—and of addressing the Dependent Variables at this point in the industry process—is much more profound.

**The simple fact** is that if the kind of failures and glitches and inconsistencies that the POR is designed to discover and adjust are permitted to persist as the product goes into massive, full-scale production, the company is already in serious trouble even if product imperfections are eventually detected at the end of the production line. Problems must be caught before they can assume **such magnitude**, and the proper phase for such detection is in pre-build and small manufacture.

*Pre-Build Manufacture.* Due to the fact that the SPC and TQC systems had already been in place for several years before the POR was introduced, most Computer companies both in North America and abroad have arranged Pre-Build facilities. Not all companies have set aside a whole building for that purpose, like Compaq's Building 5P, but an area of from 1,000 to 2,000 square feet will be set off, perhaps in the much more spacious building where full-scale manufacture will take place. The area is enclosed because the pre-build is a secret operation. The Pre-Build area is equipped with a conveyor belt and with whatever staff and machines are required for assembly and inspection. Suppliers deliver the key components of the projected product to this site, which offers an initial opportunity to determine if suppliers are able to meet their commitments with regard to deadlines, quantity and quality of components.

**The process begins** at one end of the conveyor belt, starting with the major components such as motherboard, chassis cover, metal computer base, power supply, hard drive and **DVD**. Minor components are added, and both hand and machine operated assembly procedures are accomplished as the belt moves along, and the "**finished**" unit is boxed at the other end. Once boxed, the product is opened, and the procedure is repeated in reverse—in other words, a **Root-Cause check** is completed. If an issue or error is located, it is identified and a solution is proposed if that is possible, and the unit is built again, making the necessary corrections.

**This entire process** may be repeated four or five times, depending on the nature and number of problems encountered. The Independent Variables involved in Pre-Build manufacture are (in the order discussed) <u>R</u>, <u>O</u>, <u>N</u>, <u>V</u> and <u>W</u>.

[It will be noted that there is some overlapping of Independent Variables especially in regard to Pre-Build and Small Manufacture.]

**Independent Variable <u>R</u>**, the Manufacturing Verification Strategy Pilot, ties in with the Independent Variable, the CPU, and Manufacturing Test Strategy. (manufacture pilots)—that is, components delivered as per arrangement by various suppliers—are checked to verify product stability and readiness for production, and to verify manufacturing readiness to ramp production. At the **Verification Strategy Pilot stage**, the **POR designates** the following **Deliverables**:

1. Build revenue able systems using production tooling.

2. Build initial service spaces.

3. Perform final production validation and audit.

4. Perform product integrity audit.

5. Refine and finalize manufacturing processes and tooling.

6. Train manufacturing line personnel.

7. Perform system final article inspection.

**If it becomes necessary** to revise the design documentation, the **POR designates** the following Deliverables:

1. Insure that systems and options fulfill internal unit requests.

2. **Service spares** to support internal unit requests.

3. Release production tooling and processes.

**When one or both** (if needed) of the above assessments are completed, the POR then requires the following procedures:

1. Train manufacturing line personnel.

2. Conduct program POR review.

3. Identify goal attainment.

4. Review overall readiness of product, tooling, and processes for ramp production phase.

**Following the foregoing directives** for assessment helps to insure the availability of the component (at least to some extent), its quality and functionality, whether it actually works with other components to fulfill the expectations of the original design and whether the tools, accessories and machines necessary for its incorporation are available on the assembly line. Obviously, a number of the above assessments also apply to small manufacture.

# Quality Goals

Independent Variable <u>O</u> has to do with setting up and assessing Factory Equipment and ties in with the Independent Variable, Factory Equipment Tools Defined and Ordered. While many decisions with regard to tools and equipment are made early in Pre-Build, this assessment may be ongoing throughout Pre-Build and Small Manufacture; it is crucial, however, that the assessment be complete and Equipment and Tools be correctly defined and ordered prior to full-scale manufacture.

**Two factors are significant** in addressing **Independent Variable <u>O</u>** effectively. **First**, it must be identified, and it must be demonstrated that each tool or piece of equipment is in compliance with the established goals. Each product (tool or piece of equipment) has defined rate goals for PCA and CPU manufacturing sites. It is recommended, but not required, that the gate calculator be used as a guideline in establishing the CPU goals. A product's (tool or piece of equipment) inability to meet the applicable defined quality goal has a direct impact on the anticipated costs and cycle times for that particular item.

In addition, such failure is an early indicator of field performance and may herald increased complications down the line. **Second**, Adjustments must be made according to established protocol, and **undiagnosed issues must not be permitted to accumulate**. For instance, adjustments for issues for which root-cause has been identified and verified will be accepted. However, adjustments will not be accepted for issues related to known failure modes of subassemblies currently in production. Adjustments are based upon engineer judgment and are not considered automatic and will be documented. Prompt attention to undiagnosed first-pass manufacturing line product failure is essential, such issues are reviewed per daily volume. It should be noted that unresolved issues residing in repair queues lead to a false sense of security and pose a high risk that a root-cause issue is being shipped. To this end, each board return repair queue is managed to a level that prevents issues from being shipped.

**In order to prevent** the accumulation of unresolved issues, board return repair queues are kept at or below the defined level of three times the first-pass fall out goals, multiplied by the scheduled daily volume. The exception would be if

71

root-cause diagnosis has been carried out, corrective actions verified, and the queues contain boards awaiting implementation of the corrective action.

**Independent Variable N** is the Product Volume Validation Pilot, which impacts on the Independent Variable having to do with **Projected Volumes**. Prior to entering the product validation phase, a full functionality of hardware and firmware is demonstrated against the product specification. The intent of this process is to insure that verification of each CPU level of functionality of the system has been performed. Full hardware functionality would include the following: production stepping of ASIC tested/verified on PCAs; actual storage devices (to be shipped with SKUs) operation verified; operation of keyboards and other I/O devices verified; all expansion slots' functionality verified; each memory slot functionality verified; hardware features to support product definition verified; and power management/energy star compliance features verified. The preceding process insures that each and every hardware (system and PCA level) feature has been verified and minimizes pilot verification build and future wide area testing.

**Independent Variable N involves** some overlapping **with Independent Variable O**, with the result that in actual practice time-frames may be somewhat blurred. Long-lead time components are identified and ordered per the TLT (Fixed Lead Time) defined in the materials; such identification and ordering is done independent of any phase.

Items are ordered within the appropriate time to ensure production quantities at production start. If a component is a new part or from a new vendor, strategic ordering allows for evaluation through the qualification process. This involves the building of fully functional systems (Engineering pilots) to validate the component's conformance to product and user requirements and to demonstrate manufacturability readiness.

**In keeping with POR guidelines**, the Deliverables are as follows:

1.  Build sufficient systems (with heavy engineering involvement) to support the requirements of the product validation phase; as has already been stated, the usual number of units assembled in Pre-Build is fifty.

2.  Execute test plans including wide area test, reliability test, and EMI.

3.  Resolve issues, finalize user and factory diagnostics.

4.  Perform **component first article inspections**.

5.  Revise design documentation to reflect production part versions.

6.  Finalize user documentation.

**With the foregoing check-points** duly addressed, major steps in the Pre-Build process can be taken: refining manufacturing processes, training trainers, finalizing software implementation, refining and building factory test tooling, submitting agency documentation and establishing customer support and training requirements.

In **connection with these steps**, the **POR mandates** the following Deliverables:

1. Test reports should be completed.

2. Agency grants and approvals should be complete.

3. Revised designs should be released to documentation, databases and Bills of Material.

4. One system should be identified that reflects the ability to build a revenueable unit.

5. Production tooling should be complete.

6. Long-lead risk material orders should be placed.

7. Final diagnostics—manufacturing, service, and end user—should be released.

8. The program Plan Of Record (POR) review should be conducted.

9. There should be a review of goal attainment, the production ramp plan, and the overall readiness of the product for pre-build procedure.

**Independent Variable V̲**, Pilot Verification (PVB), which impacts the Independent Variable, Final Acceptance and Quality Feedback System, and Independent Variable W̲. Test and Root Cause, which impacts—as has already been explained—the Independent Variable, Calibration and Gauging Repeatability and Reproductively, work very much in conjunction because they are part of a system that feeds back to A̲ and the Plan of Record Survey Checklist crucial information that enables the Pre-Build crew—or even the staff in Planning and Design—to correct or modify problems with components and their assembly, tools and equipment, and other inadequacies with regard to manufacture.

The **value of PVB builds is**, of course, that small quantities are involved—and this means that failures are not as detrimental to the company as would be the case if they occurred in full-scale manufacture. However, a pre-build crew has to maintain particular vigilance. Because PVB builds involve limited numbers of units—less than fifty as a rule—it is sometimes difficult to grasp the true impact that a problem that is not understood and, hence, not resolved could have on full-scale manufacturing. The potential is, in fact, overwhelming given steep manufacturing ramp and the material positions that are required to support that ramp.

Indeed, problems or issues may occur that cannot be duplicated (**CND**), and in such cases analysis is difficult if not impossible. However, it is essential that high-hour failures be resolved. Failures occurring in builds at high-hour intervals are indicative of serious problems that will prevent continuous production when larger quantities are run.

Such failures are also leading indicators of intermittent problems or longer-term reliability issues, which would cause serious reverberations if they turn up in the field. To ensure the start up with minimal risk of production stoppages due to recurrences of both normal and high-hour failures such as may have been seen in previous builds, these issues must be analyzed to root-cause and resolved. Independent Variable $\underline{W}$, Test and Root Cause, is as has been explained a procedure that occurs—or, more accurately, one can say it **begins**—at the far end of the conveyor belt with the finished, boxed unit. In Pre-Build assembly, the boxed product is then opened, noting whether arrows, lettering and directions are correctly in place and whether the product is suitably protected and can be removed as per instructions; once unboxed, the unit is sent back down the assembly-line in the opposite direction and is inspected at each assembly point—a matter of testing and tracing whatever issues may arise to root causes. This procedure may be followed four or five times if issues continue to arise. For the purpose of discussing how the POR (**Plan of Record**) was implemented in the Pre-Build Manufacture phase of the industry process, it has been useful to concentrate on its application in terms of certain of the Independent Variables that must be addressed if computer companies—in this study Compaq and its suppliers and vendors, Subject **Companies D, H and I**—are to avoid costly fallout in full-scale manufacture or long term negative consumer response. **By way of summary**, in Compaq Computer Corporation's Building 5P the following tasks are required to be effectively completed:

(1) Build sufficient (typically 5-25) systems using prototype tooling and unreleased documentation to meet the system integration phase requirements, execute test plans and resolve issues, evaluate conformance, ensure functional stability, revise design documentation as needed, build and test revised parts, demonstrate EMI (emission tests) safety and environmental compliance.

(2) Revise component and assembly documentation data bases and Bills of Material, as well as test reports, ensure Diagnostics for manufacturing, service and end user, make ready product validation pilot tooling, component assembly and tests, and **identify long-lead risk material orders** that are placed.

(3) Conduct supplier qualification reviews; program POR reviews, goal attainment, performance and cost; analyze schedule and resources, tooling plan, product transition plan and deployment plan; examine risks, opportunities and market assessment of product viability; consider the overall readiness of the product design for the product validation pilot phase in terms of quality goals.

**For the purpose of the Core Team's study**—and to facilitate the long-term implementation of the POR—it was essential to conduct a Site Pilot, or Pre-Build manufacture for each of the Subject Companies, **D, H and I**. In the case of these companies, none of which was located in North America, the Site Pilot, designed to provide verification prior to manufacturing, provided a learning experience with regard to the product and supporting processes.

The **build quantity** was kept low due to the fact that the units were non-revenue. By having an equivalent line ready for Manufacturing Verification Build (MVB), the revenueable build for personnel training, line balance and assembly, and test and software downloads equipment are validated/adjusted before ramp begins. Prior to the first MVB build, each potential area requiring a manufacturing test, such as PCA, ICT, PCA FBT, CPU pre test, and CPU run-in, CPU FPIA comply with the manufacturing test requirements as documented in the Test Matrix. Test designs and test software were verified against the test requirements. Therefore, the ICT met coverage requirements for PCAs as verified by analysis of fault injection results. It is important to point out that both at home (in North America) and abroad, Compaq offers a **Quality Training Core Curriculum**. The courses offered and their content depends on the status of the intended audience. Courses offered include problem solving, improvement processes, improvement processes using data analysis, repeatable processes, and facilitation and lead meetings. In order to provide such courses it is necessary to address issues such as management commitment and involvement, internal versus external trainers and specialists, additional Core courses needed, pulled versus required training, standardized versus company training, and the resources required for presenting the courses.

The **elements for training** are driven by and linked to relevant business needs. In terms of **Subject Companies D, H and I**, the Core Team discovered that it was often more workable to provide training only to those employees who needed it specifically to perform their designated jobs—and that the training should be given immediately prior to its on-the-job use. Language differences and procedural differences tied in with beliefs and customs peculiar to the manufacturing site were involved in this training adjustment. It was also essential that both the content and manner of the training be understood, supported and measured by management at any given site.

**Tests, measurements and assessments** have been designated at every stage of Pre-Build manufacture, so it is probably desirable at this point to provide additional information and clarification with regard to the nature and application of the plans, documents and tests that are related to industry Pre-Build. The Bill of Materials (**BOMs**) is a structured materials plan loaded less than five months before production (phase independent). The Bill of Materials (BOMs) consists of files that contain the indented structure of all materials, which make up the product. Each component part number is utilized, and its quantity per each assembly is listed along with other relevant information such as revision and affectivity dates. The Manufacturing Requirements Schedule is a file that is revised monthly to reflect the demand and supply quantities for the life of the product. These files are multiplied against each other on a monthly basis to generate the Material Requirements Plan.

This plan then generates buy sheets for each component commodity based on the delta between stock on hand and incremental requirements at the lead time offsets for each component. Each project team creates a BOM Structure and Materials Plan that are loaded accurately at less than five months prior to production.

**Long lead time component orders** are required. Test diagnostics are 99% of planned production coverage. Thus, it should be noted that all potential areas requiring a manufacturing test must comply with the manufacturing test requirements within 99% of planned test coverage as documented in the preliminary release of the Test Matrix. The Test Matrix is verified with fixture functionality and test software against the test requirements by test development and manufacturing diagnostic engineers/technicians. This provides opportunity for corporate operations and engineering to validate diagnostics and test equipment. These cautionary measures provide high confidence in the likelihood that 100% test coverage will be in place for the next phase, and give early feedback to Design and Planning with regard to potential product and component issues. A Ramp Plan is completed on both CPU and PCA. The Ramp consists of the initial 60-90 days of worldwide production.

**Constraints on the Ramp** include but are not limited to the following: factory capacities, learning curve, vendor, commitments on allocated commodities, new technology feature availability, etc. **Ramp Plans** are a required part of any project in order to ensure sufficient factory and vendor capacities or to identify areas of conflict early enough to avoid a negative impact on the project. Material orders are made, and accurate volume requirements are needed to preclude material shortages/obsolescence. Long lead components are ordered per factory lead-time (phase independent).

The Manufacturing Process Flow definition is needed in order to: drive consistency, line by line, site by site; determine new process requirements; define assembly equipment and tooling requirements; determine test strategy and test tooling requirements; define product cycle time; determine labor hours and line staffing requirements; determine capacity requirements and Ramp Plan; define BOM structures; and to define SPC and data collection requirements.

A Manufacturing Test Strategy is defined for both PCA and CPU. A Preliminary Test Matrix is defined showing locations of all required tests. The matrix will break down to show specifically which feature or function is tested at each station. This document is then used by the test development engineers and manufacturing diagnostics engineering staff in the definition and design of their tests and test stations. The test strategy is defined prior to the first tested system that is built in order to allow the test development engineers and manufacturing diagnostics engineer's adequate time to designate and develop their testers and tests. This allows the sites time to review the plan and to provide necessary feedback as to the adequacy and feasibility of implementing the strategy at each location. Test strategies are required in assessing first-pass-fallout estimates, defining assembly processes, providing a basis for test time estimates, ensuring a quality read-point for system integration and pilot verification builds, and in ensuring a downstream effective ramp.

[Note: that the System Integration Plan will involve fully functional systems (prototypes) and execute test plans to demonstrate conformance to requirements.] The procurement engineer will ensure that prototypes delivered to product design teams have this test mode implemented and working. Comprehensive testing at ICT is necessary to allow implementation of more efficient test strategies, which minimize test requirements and, thus, the cost of effective test coverage.

**Testing at ICT also serves to benefit customers** as well as the design teams who utilize tested builds in order to supply wide area testing of units. Test development engineering will supply definitions of required documentation or vector sets necessary for the development of manufacturing tests. The **procurement engineer** will provide this set of definitions to the vendor and will ensure compliance with these requirements: design; specify and breadboard/model the product components; prepare documentation and databases needed to fabricate components. Deliverables connected with the forementioned procedures are:

1.  Design mechanical and electrical components, assembles, and software, PCBs, ASICs, PCAs, Plastics, and Sheet Metal.

2.  Design and code firmware, utilities, and applications.

3.  Specify and begin qualification of major procured components, panel, keyboard, pointing device, battery, disks, and operating systems.

4.  Perform analysis on assemblies, serviceability, test and EMI compliance.

5.  Develop product tests and test plans.

6.  Begin activities including involvement of manufacturing teams, diagnosis, material sizing, user documentation, product engineering documentation and third part applications.

7.  Documentation, Bill of Material, Databases need to be fabricated or procured to obtain components, assemblies, and SKUs.

8.  Documentation of new processes.

9.  Supplier selections should be completed.

10. Bread-boarding, mockups, modeling, simulations and other verifications and design analyses should be completed.

11. Tests and tools should be used to execute the system integration phase test plans, and a new parts list should be generated.

12. Conduct design and supplier reviews and a POR review for product requirements, schedule and resources, risks and opportunities, critical material risks, purchase plan, overall completeness of design, tooling plan and deployment plan. Prior to the first MVB build, the Test Matrix is to be complete, approved and signed-off by corporate Product Engineering, and released to level A by Test Engineering Documentation Control. The extensive testing, measurement, and assessment indicated above has as its primary purpose finding and eliminating or providing solutions for issues (problems, errors)

in design, assembly or manufacturing processes before the product goes into full-scale manufacture. It is as essential to handle such issues (problems, errors) in a thorough and orderly manner, as it is to be thorough and orderly in testing for them. Statistical Process Controls (SPC) methods are used to limit the repair queues as long as the SPC is per standard approved operating procedures. **CND** issues, even when related to test-revealed problems, are to be tracked as diagnosed issues.

**Basic TQC methods** may be employed as well. When the number of **CNDs** related to a common failure code becomes a major fallout (>.5%) for the product, a formal action plan must be initiated to determine the root-cause of the failure. Root-cause determination is not necessary before the volume phase if the fallout was due to a common failure mode. However, should the issue be serious enough to generate more than .5% fallout, the project team should give careful consideration to the decision to forego root-cause determination. Undiagnosed failures >.5% of daily volume in CPU repair queues tend to hide issues which may wind up being shipped or which may be constraining production. Therefore, in order to fully understand all issues, CPU repair queues are managed to a level no greater than .3 times the fallout goals times the daily production schedule volume. Should the level of undiagnosed CPUs which have failed Testing rise above this limit, production should be suspended until the queues can be managed within the limit and corrective actions put in place to prevent reoccurrence of the issues identified. CPUs, which have been diagnosed to the root-cause and are awaiting repair are not to be counted in the determination of the limit.

The **foregoing precautions**, observed at the Pre-Build and Small Manufacture levels, minimize substantially the number of product imperfections that hamper full-scale manufacture.

*Small Manufacture.* In Building 5P, a large room is set aside for Small Manufacture, carefully equipped to create an accurate manufacturing environment—that is, it anticipates exactly the conditions of full-scale manufacture. In sites provided by Subject **Companies D, H and I**, areas for Pre-Build and Small Manufacture were set aside in large, open buildings where most of the space was devoted to full-scale manufacture. Generally speaking, a space involving from 5,000 to 8,000 square feet was designated for Small Manufacture. It is usual to limit Small Manufacture to 200 to 300 (usually revenueable) pieces or units. Pre-Build and Small Manufacture has basically the same purpose: to single out and find solutions for product and industry process issues (problems, errors) before committing to full-scale manufacture.

There is **considerable emphasis** on these two phases in the POR. Although such clarification may be to some extent an over-simplification, it is reasonably correct to say that big problems are caught in Pre-Build and smaller, more detailed issues emerge in Small Manufacture. For instance, in Pre-Build it may be discovered that the chassis cover does not actually fit or that a given component lacks certain specifications required by the design. In Small Manufacture, on the other hand, it may be discovered that a screw used to bolt down the mother board, though seemingly in place, may eventually loosen or short something out; or perhaps that a cable between the mother board and the hard drive works for the moment but may get too tight and cause problems for the customer.

A **well-monitored Small Manufacture** would probably have caught the loose connector that plagued the legendary Apple III. In other words, Pre-Build and Small Manufacture function conjointly to weed out and remedy a wide range of issues (problems, errors, miscalculations). In the Small Manufacture phase, **the POR provides** guidance in addressing Independent Variables $\underline{E}$, $\underline{S}$, $\underline{C}$, $\underline{Q}$, $\underline{H}$, $\underline{D}$, $\underline{P}$ and $\underline{M}$ (listed in order of discussion). Independent Variable $\underline{E}$, Product Validation Components Pilot, impacts on Dependent Variable, **CTO and BTO** Business Components. **Independent Variable $\underline{E}$** calls for building full-function systems (Engineering Pilots) to validate component to product and user requirements and to demonstrate manufacturers' readiness.

**Independent Variable $\underline{E}$** involves identifying, during the Test phase, the risk of component (PCB) rework or manufacturing and ship-hold requirements—details that would impact costs due to unscheduled factory downtime and labor variances. Orders for components per fixed lead-times should be completed.

With the **BOMs** structured before production, the net requirements are met for each commodity. This should ensure that manufacturing will not be impacted by material shortages. The net quantity of components are ordered outside the fixed lead-time to ensure delivery by the date of need. It is important, too, that no unverified changes be without closure. In response to manufacturing and product-related issues, the Development organizations—Test Engineering, Diagnostic Engineering and Product Engineering—will initiate changes to the product in order to resolve those issues. It then becomes necessary to ensure that those solutions correct the original problem and do not cause other problems. Therefore, as has been indicated, any changes should be verified. The appropriate personnel involved with verification, as well as the form which such verification will take, will depend on the type of change being initiated.

**Independent Variable S**, Verification System Diagnostic Process, is related to Independent Variable, Testing and Diagnostic System. Independent Variable S involves the use of both the tool and the process in a production representative environment.

The **product Verification Process**, as well as any process change between product validation and manufacturing verification, impacts methods, machine placement programs, process tooling, and/or assembly processes. Estimates of labor standards for both PCA and CPU assembly are calculated and communicated to each site. Concurrence on the estimates is reached with each site, specifically with operations and design teams.

The estimates are validated in the MVB and are then set after the first ten days of ramp. Detailed Ramp Plans are generated and communicated to each site involved in the ramp. Detailed Ramp Plans include number of lines starting at each site, start data of each line, duration of run-time for each line, and estimated daily output. Process tooling and test tooling plans should be communicated and agreed to by Operations, Engineering and by each site. Tooling plans include total number of lines tooled at each site; type and quantity of tools required for each line, and spares strategy. A Site Readiness Checklist should be completed. Each manufacturing site involved in the deployment of the product should complete all items of the Site Readiness Checklist up to the product validation phase prior to starting the Manufacturing Verification Build.

The **completion of the checklist** will ensure that the site is adequately prepared to build the projected product. The **checklist includes** documentation, preliminary labor standards, and process verification and training—and to that end, training plans must be completed. Development of human resources is an element of a successful product launch. Training plans are thus formulated and completed prior to entering the Manufacturing Verification phase for each organization when specific skills and knowledge are required by the designated project. This includes, but is not limited to, site training for PCA and CPU operations, field service, product engineering, and sales force training. Each training plan should include the timing, content and resources required to execute the training.

The **plan includes details** relating to the instruction and preparation of general trainers and on-the-job trainers. Wide-Area Testing must be complete prior to starting a revenueable production. In fact, testing is not limited to what might specifically be defined as Wide-Area Test (**WAT**) but includes integration testing as defined in the Product Test Plan established by the Core Team, as well as

Regression Testing performed on each product iteration that is intended for revenue production.

**Independent Variable $\underline{C}$**, Localization, has been discussed in connection with Planning and Design. As was suggested in that discussion, dealing with a worldwide market necessitates careful attention to the specific needs and limitations and possibilities of a given locality—and from the standpoint of Planning and Design this may mean both drastic and subtle modifications in the product being manufactured for sale in that particular geographical area.

**Localization** is likewise a significant concern at the manufacturing level. The matter of power source and voltage has been mentioned as an example of inconsistencies that must be noted and dealt with from one locale to another—and such an inconsistency would affect manufacture as well as design. In **North America**, for instance, the voltage for power sources is between 115-120, but in Latin American countries, building may be customarily done with different voltages—and in Europe the customary voltage is 220. It is essential therefore to determine whether such Localization peculiarities pose issues with regard to manufacturing: will the machines on the assembly line work on the available voltage, for instance? Labor practices, the backgrounds and belief systems of workers, even seasonal and weather conditions peculiar to a given locale can severely impact manufacture.

**Independent Variables $\underline{Q}$**, Ramp Production Processes, impacts on the Independent Variable, Manufacturing Process Flow System for PCA. Independent Variable $\underline{Q}$ calls for each site to begin producing and shipping customer systems and options at a specified ramp rate. For this industry phase the Deliverables are:

1.  Build service spare parts.

2.  Build revenueable systems at specified rates and sites.

3.  Start-up tooling and factory lines.

4.  Execute run-in test reduction plan.

5.  Start-up suppliers to volume rate.

6.  Balance manufacturing production lines.

7.  Refine test tooling and processes.

8.  Establish field return data feedback from internal unit requests.

9.  Transition engineering responsibility from design to production engineering.

10. Conduct program postmortem meeting at end of manufacturing ramp production phase.

**In connection with the last procedure**, Deliverables are:

1. Service spare parts, Customer systems and options (shipped at specified rate).

2. Conduct POR program review.

3. Identify attainment goals, open issues, plans for upgrades to design, tooling and processes.

4. Evaluate postmortem, summary and process improvement plans.

**Independent Variable H**, Training, which impacts on Dependent Variable Quality Training Requirements has already been examined in detail in connection with Pre-Build Manufacture and applies at every level or phase of the industry process.

**Independent Variable D**, Manufacturing Verification Pilot, impacts the Dependent Variable System Volume Expectations and Transition Plan. This Variable calls for the manufacture of revenueable systems (Manufacturing Pilots) to verify product stability and readiness for production and to verify manufacturing readiness to ramp production. It provides **a double-check** with regard both to how well the assembled components have come together to meet original specifications and to the extent to which the assembled product, as it stands, can be anticipated to meet production goals.

**Independent Variable P**, Manufacturing Verification, impacts on the Dependent Variable having to do with the structuring of the Bill of Materials (BOM), which has already been identified and discussed at some length. The Manufacturing Verification is a revenue build and as such it requires that all BOMs, parts and sub-assemblies be released to rev. A. PCAs are to be available to support the CPU build. It may be necessary to build MVB PCAs while the CPU is still in the product validation phase; therefore, it is required that PCA BOMs be **released to revision A**. (Delivery of part not in lead-time of CPU requirements). Manufacturing and purchasing would be impacted if any part is not at revision A. (e.g. Po's) because parts could not be placed and fulfilled, nor could they be received and the appropriate steps in the supplier process completed.

**Full functionality** to product specification must be proven prior to PCB ordering, with PCB lead-times ranging from six to eight weeks and the PCA MRS lead-time offset from the CPU, MRS. Each PCB is ordered with confidence that no artwork changes have been effected before use in production to preclude rework, scrap, obsolescence schedule and capacity impacts. Program Risks is the Dependent Variable impacted by **Independent Variable M**, Program Risk Assessment Complete. Through facilitation by operations planning, the various functional groups and manufacturing sites assess the product and process performance of the project through ramp prior to entering the volume phase. Elements that are assessed are product holds, product yields, major causes for failures, labor standards, ramp time scale/throughput and any required and outstanding corrective actions. The impact to manufacturing if this procedure were not carried out is a potentially problematic product/process that does not meet projected goals.

*Full Scale Manufacture.* Because of the painstaking assessments, testing and measurements during Pre-Build and Small Manufacture and the analysis of the data that such procedures provide, the computer companies—Compaq and the Subject Companies D, H and I—went into full-scale manufacture with most of the information necessary for successful high-volume production solidly in place. For the most part, therefore—with the exception of **Independent Variable T**—Dependent Variables need not be addressed in connection with Full-Scale Manufacture. To the extent that this does, indeed, prove to be the case, to that extent the methods prescribed first by SPC and then TQC and finally by the POR are demonstrated to be successful.

In connection with the above preliminary procedures, **Full Scale Manufacturing Readiness** is indicated by the resolution of all stop ship issues. Stop ship issues are defined as priority one (an issue and problem enhancement tracking system) and any issue that is viewed as having the potential of being a major customer dissatisfier. In order to proceed into **full-scale manufacture**, the product is not to contain any unresolved priority one issues. A **corporate operations engineering** representative is to review the open defects list of issues and participate in the review meeting in order to fully understand the open issues.

However, a lower level assembly build may begin if a priority one issue is identified and the technical evaluation has determined that the root-cause of the issue is not the build assembly. The impact to manufacturing is that a stop ship issue detected during the manufacturing process will result in the generation of a product hold. The **activities associated with its containment** and the appropriate corrective action will have an impact on the ability to meet production goals. It is therefore essential to make certain that all agency approvals have been granted.

**Independent Variable T**, Ramp Production System, which ties in with the Dependent Variable, Ramp Plan System, is related to full-scale manufacturing readiness. This Variable involves beginning to produce and ship customer systems and options at a specified product goal ramp rate, demonstrating compliance to quality goals. Each product has defined rate goals for PCA site and CPU sites. **It is recommended**, not required, that the gate calculator be used as a guideline in establishing the CPU goals. Adjustments for issues for which root-cause has been identified and verified are accepted. Adjustments will not be accepted for issues related to known failure modes of subassemblies currently in production. Adjustments should be based upon an engineer judgment and not considered automatic; they will thus be documented.

A product's inability to meet the **defined quality goal** has a direct impact on the anticipated costs and cycle times that have been projected. In addition, such failure is an early indicator of field performance. Engineering pilot failures discovered during the Manufacturing Verification Build must have root-cause determined, corrective action identified and implemented in order to proceed with the ramp phase. The resolution criteria is achieved by detailing the failure on a quality waiver and gaining agreement to ship from upper management. **EP testing** is in place to ensure that the product will **meet the customers' expectations**. If the test is incomplete, there are risks of process and product-related failures in the field. Additionally, false failures may slant the quality indices and adversely impact the ship readiness decision for a new product. As is the case at every phase or level of the industry process, training implementation must be emphasized.

*Training manufacturing personnel should be completed before* a state of **readiness** is assumed. The training plans developed for the program and each manufacturing site are implemented in the ramp phase. This includes, but is not limited to, training on new assembly processes, new technologies, and product awareness. In general, with regard to **Manufacturing and Deployment**, second quarter mainstream will be built by a specific selected company that will deploy chassis and final assemblies that will be regionalized to maximize lead-time and shipping costs. **Shipping Internet Computer Products Globally** involves special considerations. The product must meet internationally recognized standards and be kept marked (labeled) to reflect compliance with the specifications for safety and electrical integrity (e.g. low electromagnetic-magnetic emissions and high immunity against external electrical noise). The majority of industrial countries have developed their own equipment compliance standards—or they accept standards developed by some other country or countries. The product that is submitted for, and granted, approval needs to be representative of that which will be manufactured in production.

The **impact to manufacturing**, should a product fail to be accorded approval, is potential scrap, rework and obsolescence of those parts or sub-assemblies that need to be modified/replaced to attain compliance. Hence, building a product ahead of approval could increase the quantity of products affected, as well as the complexity of any potential rework, inventory logistics and holding costs. **Depending on material lead-time**, changing over to new parts or sub-assemblies will result in schedule delays.

For these reasons, compliance to quality goals must be demonstrated. Compliance means that quality goals have been established and met. Each product will have defined FPF rate goals for lPCA composite and CPU composite. Other measures that are to be taken as a part of full-scale manufacture include **Packaging and Life Cycle Model.**

Packaging will follow the specifications for retail packaging. The following product volumes were used for planning purposes in handling the product under manufacture during the Core Team's initial implementation of the POR (Note that planned flexibility should account for 30%. Volumes by SKU are tracked in detail through the life cycle model process): "Build plan is: USA—May—27,355, June—136,775, July—246,195, August—136,770, total = 547,100, 55% of volume. Canada—May—3,470, June—1,730, July—31,230, August—17,350, total = 69,400, 7% of volume. Latin America—May—3,230, June—16,175, July—29,115, August—16,175, total = 64,700, 6% of volume. Europe—May—10,800, June—4,000, July—97,200, August—4,000, total = 216,000, 22% of volume. Asia—May—2,430, June—12,175, July—21,915, August—12,175, total 48,700, 5% of volume. Japan—May—2,705, June—13,525, July—24,340, August—13,525, total = 54,100, 5% of volume. The profit goal utilizing Plan Of Record (POR) is 16% overall life cycle gross margin (monitor included).

During the **initial implementation of the Plan of Record** (POR), the Core Team gave only cursory attention to Full-Scale Manufacture (at least in terms of its on-site processes and procedures). **A primary intent of the POR and the PORI** (Plan of Record Index) was and is to identify and eliminate problems before a product begins the full-scale production phase.

Therefore, the assumption was that if the **POR and PORI** were indeed effective assessment and informational tools, Full-Scale Manufacture would proceed smoothly. Once a product goes into full-scale manufacture it enters that scary no-man's-land where it is "**out of the hands**" of planners, designers, testers and analysts—and where failures in those early phases manifest themselves (multiplied by hundreds and thousands) in fallouts, shut-downs, unmet quotas and deadlines and, ultimately, in various kinds of customer dissatisfaction once the finished product is shipped and sold. To some extent, the Full-Scale Manufacture phase was, for the Core Team as for others in the companies involved, a period of waiting until "the results were in," so to speak.

Historically, the industry trend had been to regard the boxing and shipping of the finished product when it came off the assembly line as the **end** of the industry process. The product was launched; it was sent out to seek its fortune and the company's fortune as best it could, given presumably the best efforts of all company departments involved in its making. However, the POR and PORI are designed on **the premise that there is no end to the industry process**—which the process is not linear but circular and that product improvement can be immediate and ongoing. On the basis of this premise, Marketing and Customer Service are significant phases of the industry process.

# Marketing and Customer Service: Implementing Dependent Variables

From the beginning, and probably due to the nature of that beginning, personal computer companies have had a strange relationship with consumers. The hobbyists who assembled the first personal computers had in mind that their creations would appeal primarily to others like themselves who wanted to experiment with components and see what marvels they could make their combinations perform. Even when upstart personal Computer companies began to envision somewhat larger markets, they were given no encouragement from the computer industry that was already established, the makers of mainframes and minicomputers that sold to the government and industry and big businesses and universities.

"The larger computer companies were busy developing mainframes and improving computer systems for industry, and couldn't see why anyone would want a home computer. They also failed to see the implications of the new microprocessors that were small and cheap" (*A Science Odyssey* 1). However, as this article goes on to assert, "From a do-or-die business venture in the 1970s, the personal computer evolved from a sophisticated toy for electronics enthusiasts to an even more sophisticated—but easier to use—household and workplace commodity." Thus, from the outset, computer companies were dealing with an unexpected, a surprise market. In 1981, IBM—like other large companies, slow at first to respond to the possibility of a general market for the small, less expensive computers—introduced its personal computer (PC) for use in the home, office and schools, and the 1980s saw an expansion in computer use in all three arenas as clones of the IBM PC made the personal computer even more affordable. As **LaMorte and Lilly point out**, "The number of personal computers in use more than doubled from 2 million in 1981 to 5.5 million in 1982. Ten years later, 65 million PCs were being used"(LaMorte & Lilly, 6). But the fact that there was a burgeoning general market for PCs did not mean that there were hordes of contented consumers.

Many people who joined the "**PC craze**" were intimidated by the machines, fearful of pressing the wrong key and losing whole programs or of unwittingly damaging the machine. **Computer viruses** created anxiety in customers who were enticed by online possibilities.

As **Les Freed states**, "For consumers, the late 1980s were a time of frustration. No sooner had they learned to run their new PCs and Macs than a new, better, larger, faster model was on the shelf. New versions of software, printers, and modems made it impossible to have the latest of everything" (Freed, 9). Mind-boggling changes continued, of course, through the 1990s. Freed continues, "Not only were hardware and software obsolete, people were also getting caught up in their own obsolescence. For years employers had included the operating systems and software names in their advertising for clerical and secretarial positions. As companies used more temporary workers and included both IBM clones and Macintosh's in their operations, proficiency with only one slammed the door on employment opportunities."

# INTERMISSION BREAK!

**Pressure in the job market and in education** resulted in situations that were fraught with tension and dissatisfaction: "Many people enrolled in classes to learn the latest software or update their computer skills. A good, well-rounded employee needed to know desktop publishing, two or more word processing programs, at least one spreadsheet program, and a graphics package. They had to be able to access the company local area network (LAN), send and receive E-mail using high-speed modems, and solve problems with hardware and software to maximize their output. Microprocessor-driven telephones, cellular phones, and pagers added to the complexity of the job, and **repetitive motion syndrome** from using keyboards hour after hour created an army of people wearing wrist braces" (Freed, 9-10). With the PC industry increasingly dominating important areas of their lives, consumers' expectations with regard to how effectively the product performed and what it was able to do became more exacting and imaginative. Nor were these consumers at all sure that they could trust the sometimes transitory, always competitive companies that advertised for their business. The very title of an article like **Walter S. Mossberg's Jan. 28, 2001 "Be on Your Guard For These 10 Lies As You Shop for a PC"** indicates a strong element of skepticism and distrust of computer companies and their products, not just on the part of the writer but his intended audience as well. A keen awareness of consumer response, much of it troublesome if not entirely negative, was what had motivated the author, and then the two Core Team members that were enlisted, to tackle developing the POR and PORI in the first place. The team had read the letters that came across their desks, had taken the phone calls and had scanned the articles in industry and trade magazines, and members were convinced that Customer Service could not be an industry after-thought, handled haphazardly and perhaps even grudgingly. The team saw the benefits of finding a way to **channel consumer feedback** directly into the industry process.

Therefore, just as the POR had prioritized the early stages, or phases, of the industry process, Planning and Design, Pre-Build and Small Manufacture—phases during which testing can be done and information obtained and acted upon—the plan the Core Team designed also prioritized the often-neglected phase involving **Customer Service** and Feedback, first because a better company-customer relationship is badly needed and secondly because this, too, is an industry phase during which tests, checks, tabulations and surveys can be conducted and in which crucial information can be obtained and routed to operations where it will be useful.

In **connection with Marketing and Customer Service and Feedback**, the following Independent Variables apply: **Independent Variable I**, Customer Impact/CSI, which relates to the Dependent Variable, Customer Satisfaction Impact System; **Independent Variable J**, CND Quality Issues and Goals, which ties in with Dependent Variable, Quality Goals and Deployment System; **Independent Variable L**, Service Operation Schedule, which obviously is an extension of Dependent Variable, Services Schedules; **Independent Variable U**, Definition and Planning Development, which impacts Dependent Variable, Material Requirements Systems Board. **Independent Variable W**, already discussed, is also related to this industry phase.

**Independent Variable I.** Acknowledge Customer Impact, previously measured by the CSI but, during the Core Team's initial implementation of the POR, measured by the PORI. The **PORI is a composite measure of customer loyalty**, which combines several individual measures of customer satisfaction and commitment. During this time, it was possible to identify customer satisfaction performance data from the four subject companies to determine an awareness of the customer satisfaction initiative. It was necessary to establish a common language and direction for this initiative, to unify efforts to focus on the customer, and to give status.

Status is identified by being complete, that is, in progress globally to be integrated into orientation. The core curriculum is problem solving, process improvement, SPC, design of experiment, design for manufacturability and service, and effective facilitation skills.

**Independent Variable J, CND Quality Issues and Goals**, which ties in with Dependent Variable Quality Goals and Deployment System, is implemented most effectively by giving adequate attention to consumer feedback, especially customer service demands that indicate problems with the product. Such responses are to be systematically tracked. If the number of CNDs related to a common failure code becomes **a major fallout (.5%)** for the product process, a formal action plan must be initiated to determine the root-cause of the failure. Beta units (field cases closed) and internal units are the first impartial read points on a new Internet personal computer product. **Root-cause** and **corrective action** must be identified for repeated issues found during Beta programs, internal unit requests and seed programs. It is necessary to respond quickly to issues identified with those units because the company runs the risk of producing volume quantities of a product that may require field level rework (that is, extensive customer service in retail or after the product is marketed), product holds, etc. Another critical aspect of **Independent Variable J** is reconciling current sales and demand projections. During the months preceding product announcement, the inputs for supply are based on product positioning, financial commitments, factory capacities, and material and technology constraints. That is, the demand and sales-out quantities are based on forecast. The purpose for the reconciliation is to ensure that build is not exceeding demand, which would result in the product being built into finished goods inventory beyond the agreed-upon inventory targets or to a degree that could cause rework and obsolescence during the product's life cycle.

Independent Variable **L**, Service Operation Schedule, which as it is implemented is a concrete manifestation of the Independent Variable which assumes that there will be some occasion for service scheduling in connection with any product, illustrates Serviceability specification, **Warranty proposal**, Documentation readiness, along with the development of "spares" kits and plans for the deployment of spare parts. Also integral to the implementation of **Independent Variable L** is Quality Service Training. A quality training roadmap is established which consists of four phases: customer satisfaction awareness, core curriculum development, and the incorporation of the foregoing in a strategic quality plan, and ongoing integration and implementation. During the initial implementation of the **POR**, the Core Team introduced the **PORI** (Plan of Record Index) as an improvement over the previously used **CSI** (Customer Satisfaction Index).

The data gathered in the PORI is the primary measure by which customer satisfaction is tracked. In customer satisfaction calculations, **the highest level** of overall satisfaction with the manufacturer and thus the most likely to repurchase and recommend the brand equals the PORI percentage number. **Loyal customers** are those who meet the **PORI/CSI** criteria of being satisfied with a brand, likely to repurchase the brand's Internet products and services, and likely to recommend the brand's Internet products and services to others. Strategies should be developed to retain loyal customers because they are more profitable for the OEM than other customers (by providing revenue growth, operating cost savings, referrals, and willingness to pay price premiums.) **Favorable customers** are those who meet some of the **PORI criteria but not all**. These customers tend to be satisfied with a brand, but are not as likely to repurchase and recommend the brand, as are loyal customers. It becomes necessary to determine why these customers, though satisfied, are not as likely to repurchase and recommend, and then to develop strategies to encourage future commitment. Customers' experience with the company evolve from various stages in the company-customer relationship: pre-purchase, purchase, on-going service and support, product service performance, and delivery and set-up. **Customers need to feel that the company understands their business and IT needs**, that it is a business partner that can be trusted, that it works hard to build customer relationships, and that it offers low cost of ownership through the life cycle of the product, including purchase, installation and maintenance. Product **Service Performance** is viewed as offering the highest quality products, delivering the **highest quality Professional Services**, offering products with the highest level of hardware reliability, providing the most prompt and responsive phone support center assistance when the customer needs it, completing contracted projects when promised, offering products with the highest level of software reliability, having a support staff with superior technical competency, and having initial hardware reliability—determined by how frequently the product arrives in full working order.

**On-going Service and Support** consists of providing the most effective resolution of service and support problems offering timely and effective problem escalation management, providing spare parts when they are needed, taking ultimate responsibility for service problems regardless of who provides the service, keeping the customer pro-actively informed about the status of the service events by providing the most effective service and support via its web-page.

The **four Subject Companies, Compaq and Companies D, H and I**, were targeted for measurement. The questions were customer-experience focused in order to examine a customer's relationship with Compaq and D, H and I at customer touch points.

Quotas were set for each brand measured to ensure sufficient sample size for meaningful statistical analysis. Each brand sample was chosen randomly from those companies with the brand installed. Data was collected in 35 countries and weighted by size of IT market. It was partly on the basis of this data that the success of the POR and PORI was determined. **Independent Variable $\underline{U}$**, Definition and Planning Development, which impacts on the Dependent Variable, Material Requirements Systems Board, is based on the conceptual user model. Product requirements are defined, design approaches are established, and engineering's product specifications are developed. **Independent Variable $\underline{U}$** reflects customer impact and involves feedback that was the **basic for the Core Team's original concept** with regard to the content and structure of the POR, and this impact and feedback constitutes what becomes a unique and significant aspect of the Plan of Record—the looping back of crucial information available at the so-called end of the industry process to what may be perceived as its beginning, Planning and Design. Deliverables and controls in both these regards are:

1. Refine user.

2. Redefine Market requirements.

3. Document and define product description and revision history.

The **product description defines** hardware, software, form factor and weight, and ease of use requirements with focus on new features. **The looping back aspect of the POR** means that Customer Requirements are available prior to entering the design phase to allow adequate time to develop new manufacturing requirements for the product:

1. New manufacturing strategy, technology/process requirements

2. Material/supplier requirements

3. Test/diagnostic requirements. **Product Revision History** includes the product name, the family of the products that will be shipped, and the accessories with which this family of products will be compatible. **Customer Requirements** define customer/user needs and wants for a new product. This includes the product description, cost and pricing targets, early announce schedule, volume milestones, and rough product volume expectations. The timing of Todd Wasserman's October 9, 2000 article, "'Customer view' defines Compaq's branding tack," is interesting in terms of the goals of the Plan of Record (POR) and its implementation. Wasserman quotes Doug Fox, Compaq svp-marketing and strategy, who explains, "Compaq is taking a cautious approach to its latest 'branding campaign, weighing consumer response before it plots long-range expansion." Fox goes on to indicate that the campaign effort had not been mapped out beyond the initial few months, with its tenure to be determined by "how much people take away," and whether it boosts sales. "Obviously we're going to track and do the basic block-and-tackling, and look at business results and fine tune it over time," Wasserman quotes Fox as saying. Wasserman goes on to note that the estimated $300 million effort was more than just a campaign; it was the first fully integrated branding effort in Compaq's history that includes not only TV and print, but packaging, public relations and even the way Compaq reps answer the phone. "Compaq is focusing the campaign

from a customer's point of view, rather than an 'inside-out approach of making broad claims'," Wasserman notes (Wasserman, l). In a more recent article, "Keeping customers happy," April 2001, Elana Harris states: "Much like Fedex, Compaq…found it needed to cater more to its customers. The previous year Compaq executives decided to embark on a service program that's resulted in a **10 percent improvement** in **customer satisfaction** scores." Harris continues, "Compaq was doing well in areas like operational performance, but interpersonal skills were weak so managers decided to focus on trying to involve customers more. **Now** Compaq service reps learn to look at customer problems in a broader sense, rather than just focusing on a specific problem. They now update customers on a job's status" (Harris, 2) Harris notes that it is important to find out what the gap is between "what you're offering and what your customer wants."

# Measuring The Success of The POR (PORI, CSI): Financial Impact

The conception, development and implementation of the POR—Plan of Record (**POR, PORI, CSI**) took place in a receptive, cooperative company climate, not only in terms of **Compaq Computer Corporation**™ (the primary focus of the plan's development and implementation) but of the **Subject Companies D, H and I as well**. Each Internet Computer Product producer has similar goals and a sincere desire to achieve business excellence in their technology segment and in customer satisfaction. As a review of the history and nature of the personal computer industry indicated, certain inherent problems existed just by virtue of the industry's unique beginnings and the mind-set of early entrepreneurs; and an examination of articles in current financial and trade journals served to emphasize the wide range of additional industry complications created by the introduction of the Internet and the World Wide Web with the resulting global market. Compaq Computer Corporation™ and the Subject Companies D, H and I readily acknowledged the significance of the basic question posed by this research: was it possible to devise a more successful production and marketing plan as it relates to strategic Computer Product Management of an IPC (Internet Personal Computer) product globally? In contemplating such a plan, other concerns were equally obvious. Could the impacting variables be identified and defined, and would it be possible to identify the implementation processes to manage an IPC from definition planning to production ramp, volume and service training? What would be the gains and opportunities for product management of an IPC with a Strategic Marketing Plan, and would such a plan impact *customer satisfaction*?—and, further, what challenges would be added to Service Operations? These were questions considered by the POR Core Team in outlining their research, and they were questions that were of immediate and pressing importance to Compaq Computer Corporation™ and Subject Companies D, H and I. "Immediate and pressing" were operative terms: given the volatile nature of the personal computer industry, especially after the introduction of the Internet and World Wide Web, answers to such questions had to be found at once.

Therefore, while there was receptiveness and cooperation, from Senior Management on down, there was also urgency—there was a need to do what could be done quickly and accurately. It has been emphasized already that the research was primarily empirical; the Plan of Record (POR) was being implemented as it was being devised and being devised as it was being implemented. Moreover, since the plan itself provided for systematic doubling back, re-checking, testing, assessing and analyzing at every phase of the industry process, it was possible to be assured, at least to some extent, of its effectiveness as the research team went along.

The **members of the POR Core Team** were, thus, reasonably certain that the methodology that is the subject within this book provides an important link in gauging management responsibility for producing quality Internet personal computer products globally; in the team's hands-on development and implementation of the POR members were reassured, at every step along the way, that they were coming up with a strategic information planning method that is appropriate, structured, controlled, documented and that can be fully understood by workers trained in the field. Testing and assessment during and at the completion of the implementation of the POR—the Plan of Record Index (PORI) and the Customer Satisfaction Index (CSI) data—demonstrated predictable results in each designated category.

# Results of PORI and CSI Data For Subject Companies C, D, H and I

Following are the scoring results in terms of percentage differences. Where no goal category is identified, that identifier is classified information. As has already been established, raw data is also classified but is included in this study in terms of assumptions, percentages, final figures and basic conclusions. Listed below, for each of the four subject companies, are the results of the **POR/PORI and CSI surveys**—matched with the strengths and opportunities for each subject company that utilized the POR instead of the methods previously used for product management and quality control. Companies are identified as **Company C (Compaq), D, H and I**. It will be noted that the percentages increase with each company when utilizing the **POR/PORI and CSI method**. These **increases in percentages clearly show a gain** within each category and demonstrate the success of the plan **POR and its elements PORI and CSI**.

**Strengths and Opportunities for company C**
Company C
*Plan of Record Performance Index*

# Plan of Record

| Readiness | Measured by: Product | Goals- | 19XX | 2XXX |
|---|---|---|---|---|
| 1. Processes | Short Delivery Cycle % | | 93% | 99% |
| 2. Product Quality | Incoming Material % | | 91% | 98% |
| 3. Market Share | Competitor % | | 34% | 43% |
| 4. Manufacture | Readiness % | | 90% | 99% |
| 5. Services | Readiness % | | 89% | 99% |
| 6. Training | Asset Utilization % | | 87% | 98% |
| 7. Program Review | Flex for Mix Changes % | | 93% | 99% |
| 8. Customer Impact | CSI % | | 79% | 90% |

# Design of Experiment

Identification of CTO and BTO POR global business components was completed.
Identification of Strategic Marketing MRD business components was completed.
List of Strategic Management Requirements was completed.
Identification Plan of Record Product Development Processes, Components completed.
Identification of Manufacturing Readiness was completed.
Identification of Quality Training Requirements was completed.
Identification of Program Review was completed.
Identification of Customer Satisfaction Impact Attributes Data was completed.

As illustrated in the foregoing chart, in the category of Product Readiness, Company C demonstrated a 6% improvement with short delivery cycles, which had a positive impact on revenue in excess of $6.8 million. Incoming Material Quality improved by 7% and had a positive impact on revenue of $11.2 million, a figure that takes into account warranty dollars. Competitor versus Market Share increased in Company C by 9% as a factor of sales, which impacted revenue and profit by $51.9 million. Manufacturing Readiness improved by 9%, which assisted in time-to-market impact affecting an increase in sales-out. Services Readiness increased by 10%, which resulted in improved customer support response and a decrease in service repair time. Training viewed as an Asset Utilization tool increased by 11%, which improved the ability to diagnose and resolve issues and concerns more punctually during the build processes and met time-to-market goals. Progress Review viewed as a Flex for Mix change increased 6%, which allowed Marketing Product Changes to meet immediate market demands and served as a learning tool to implement new features in marketing. Customer Impact, in terms of the CSI, increased by 11% as an overall customer satisfaction rating.

## Strengths and Opportunities for D
Company D
*Plan of Record Performance Index*

# Plan of Record

| Readiness | Measured by: Product | Goals | 19xx | 2xxx |
|---|---|---|---|---|
| 1. Processes | Short Delivery Cycle % | | 91% | 96% |
| 2. Product Quality | Incoming Material % | | 90% | 97% |
| 3. Market Share | Competitor % | | 30% | 38% |
| 4. Manufacture | Readiness % | | 92% | 97% |
| 5. Services | Readiness % | | 70% | 81% |
| 6. Training | Asset Utilization % | | 85% | 94% |
| 7. Program Review | Flex for Mix Changes % | | 91% | 95% |
| 8. Customer Impact | CSI % | | 54% | 90% |

# Design for Experiment

Identification of CTO and BTO POR global business components was completed.
Identification of Strategic Marketing MRD business components was completed.
List of Strategic Product Management Requirements was completed.
Identification Plan of Record Product Development Processes, Components completed.
Identification of Manufacturing Readiness was completed.
Identification of Quality Training Requirements was completed.
Identification of Program Review was completed.
Identification of Customer Satisfaction Impact Attribute Data was completed.

As illustrated in the foregoing chart, in the category of Product Readiness Company D demonstrated a 5% improvement with Short Delivery cycles, which had a positive impact on revenue in excess of $2.1 million. Incoming material quality improved by 7% and had a positive impact on revenue of $5.3 million, a figure that takes into account warranty dollars. Competitor versus Market Share increased in Company D by 8% as a factor of Sales, which impacted revenue and profit by $6.9 million. Manufacturing Readiness improved by 5%, which assisted in time-to-market impact affecting an increase in sales-out. Services Readiness increased by 11%, which resulted in improved customer support response and a decrease in service repair time. Training, viewed as an Asset Utilization tool, increased by 9%, which improved the ability to diagnose and resolve issues and concerns more quickly during the build processes and met time-to-market goals. Program Review, viewed as a Flex for Mix change, increased 4%, which allowed for marketing product changes to meet immediate market demands and served as a learning tool to implement new features for marketing. Customer Impact, in terms of the CSI, increased by 36% as an overall customer satisfaction rating.

# Plan of Record

| Readiness | Measured by: Product | Goals | 19xx | 2xxx |
|---|---|---|---|---|
| 1. Product Quality | Incoming Material % | | 93% | 96% |
| 2. Components | Material % | | 92% | 97% |
| 3. Market Share | Competition % | | 34% | 38% |
| 4. Manufacture | Readiness % | | 93% | 97% |
| 5. Services | Readiness % | | 73% | 89% |
| 6. Training | Asset Utilization % | | 93% | 95% |
| 7. Program Review | Flex for Mix Changes % | | 93% | 96% |
| 8. Customer Impact | CSI % | | 55% | 83% |

# Design of Experiment

Identification of CTO and BTO POR Global Business Components was completed.
Identification of Strategic Marketing MRD Business Components was completed.
List of Strategic Product Management Requirements was completed.
Identification Plan of Record Product Development Programs, Components, completed.
Identification of Manufacturing Readiness was completed.
Identification of Quality Training Requirements was completed.
Identification of Program Review was completed.
Identification of Customer Satisfaction Impact Attribute Data was completed.

As illustrated in the foregoing chart, in the category of Product Readiness Company H demonstrated a 3% improvement with Short Delivery Cycles that had a positive impact on revenue in excess of $1.1 million. Incoming Material Quality improved by 5% and had a positive impact on revenue of $2.4 million, a figure that takes into account warranty dollars. Competitor versus Market Share increased in Company H by 4% as a factor of sales, which impacted revenue and profit by $4.9 million. Manufacturing Readiness improved by 4%, which assisted in time-to-market impact affecting an increase in sales-out. Services Readiness increased by 16%, which resulted in improved customer support response and a decrease in service repair time. Training, viewed as an Asset Utilization tool, increased by 2%, which improved the ability to diagnose and resolve issues and concerns more quickly during the build processes and met time-to-market goals. Program Review, viewed as a Flex for Mix Change, increased 3%, which allowed for Marketing Product Changes to meet immediate market demands and served as a learning tool to implement new features for marketing. Customer impact, in terms of **CSI**, increased by 28% as an overall customer satisfaction rating.

**Strengths and Opportunities for I**
Company I
*Plan of Record Performance Index*

# Plan of Record

| Readiness | Measured by: Product | Goals | 19xx | 2xxx |
|---|---|---|---|---|
| 1. Processes | Short Delivery Cycle % | | 94% | 96% |
| 2. Product Quality | Incoming Material % | | 90% | 98% |
| 3. Market Share | Competitor % | | 30% | 39% |
| 4. Manufacturing | Readiness % | | 90% | 98% |
| 5. Services | Readiness % | | 70% | 92% |
| 6. Training | Asset Utilization % | | 88% | 91% |
| 7. Program Review | Readiness % | | 94% | 95% |
| 8. Customer Impact | CSI % | | 37% | 74% |

# Design of Experiment

Identification of CTO and BTO POR Global Business Components completed.
Identification of Strategic Marketing MRD Business Components was completed.
List of Strategic Product Management Requirements was completed.
Identification Plan of Record Product Development Processes, Components, completed.
Identification of Manufacturing Readiness was completed.
Identification of Quality Training Requirements was completed.
Identification of Program Review was completed.
Identification of Customer Satisfaction Impact Statistics Data was completed.

As illustrated in the foregoing chart, in the category of Product Readiness Company I demonstrated a 2% improvement with Short Delivery Cycles that had a positive impact on revenue in excess of $3.8 million. Incoming Material Quality improved by 8% and had a positive impact on revenue of $3.3 million, a figure that takes into account warranty dollars. Competitor versus Market Share increased in Company I by 9% as a factor of Sales, which impacted revenue and profit by $5.7 million. Manufacturing Readiness improved by 8%, which assisted in time-to-market impact affecting an increase in sales-out. Services Readiness increased by 22%, which resulted in improved customer support response and a decrease in service repair time. Training, viewed as an Asset Utilization tool, increased by 3%, which improved the ability to diagnose and resolve issues and concerns more quickly during the build processes and met time-to-market goals. Program Review, viewed as a Flex for Mix Change, increased 1%, which allowed for Marketing Product Changes to meet immediate market demands and served as a learning tool to implement new features for marketing. Customer Impact, in terms of the CSI, increased by 37% as an overall customer satisfaction rating.

Examination of the foregoing charts rating Compaq Computer Corporation[TM] and Subject Companies D, H and I in eight relevant categories indicates that the Plan of Record (POR) and its survey instrument, the Plan of Record Index (PORI), along with the CSI utilized by Company C, Compaq, constitute a new information technology tool that demonstrates a 98-99 % success rate and a clear advantage in all categories defined. In comparative analysis with companies D, H and I, it is a comprehensive and productive tool that can be implemented when producing Internet Personal Computer Products globally. Attribute Analysis Data Provided by POR, (PORI and CSI) it has been emphasized in previous chapters that a unique feature of the POR is the components PORI and CSI and is the dynamic inclusion of Customer Service and Consumer Feedback as part of the industry process and the automatic and immediate looping back or routing back of response to the "finished product" to Planning and Design. This aspect of the Plan produced significant information through Attribute Analysis Data: Number one in attribute importance globally was providing effective resolution of service and support problems.

**Number one perceptions of effective problem resolutions are driven by:**

1. Having support staff and superior technical competency.

2. Delivering the highest quality professional service.

3. Taking ultimate responsibility for service problems regardless of who provides the service.

4. Offering timely and effective problem escalation management.

5. Offering warranty terms and conditions that best meet the customers' needs.

6. Completing contracted projects when promised.

7. Providing spare parts when the customer needs them.

8. Having initial hardware reliability, measured by how frequently the product arrives in full working order.

9. Keeping the customer pro-actively informed about the status of the customer events.

**Number two in attribute importance globally was whether the personal computer company understands customers' business IT needs. Perceptions of understanding customers' business needs are driven by:**

1.  Demonstrating knowledge of IT industry solutions.

2.  Offering all the products, services and expertise necessary to provide complete IT solutions.

3.  Being a company that works hard to build customer relationships.

4.  Demonstrating knowledge of the company's full line of products and services.

5.  Being a business partner that customers can trust.

6.  Providing timely responses to the sales and product inquiries.

7.  Having the easiest web-based systems for answering the customers' needs.

8.  Keeping the customer pro-actively informed about the status of the service events.

9.  Offering the most competitive initial price on hardware and services.

10. Offering the flexibility to buy however the customer would like.

11. Offering the most complete set of product features and functionality to meet customer needs.

**Providing the best overall value for the money is number three in attribute importance globally. Perceptions of the best value for the money are driven by:**

1.  Offering the most competitive initial price on hardware and service.

2.  Having a low cost of ownership over the product's life cycle, including purchase, installation and maintenance.

3.  Offering the highest quality products.

4.  Offering products that are the most compatible within the customers' computing environment.

5.  Delivering new products that are complete and ready for installation into IT and computing environments.

6.   Having system hardware that is the easiest to upgrade.

7.   Offering the flexibility to buy according to customer preference.

8.   Offering products with the highest level of hardware reliability.

9.   Being a company that works hard to build customer relationships and provides the most effective service and support via its web page.

**Offering the highest quality products is number four in attribute importance globally. Perceptions of high quality products are driven by:**

1.   Offering products with the highest level of hardware reliability.

2.   Offering products with the highest level of software reliability.

3.   Being a business partner that can be trusted.

4.   Delivering the highest quality professional services.

5.   Providing the best overall value for the money with regard to initial hardware reliability, measured by how frequently the product arrives in full working order.

6.   Offering the most complete set of features and functionality to meet customer needs.

7.   Having products and services available when the customer wants them.

8.   Having products that are easy to integrate with other industry standard products and services.

9.   Demonstrating knowledge of information technology industry solutions.

**Number five in attribute importance globally is whether the company makes doing business with them simple and easy. Perceptions of ease in doing business are driven by:**

1.   Being a company that works hard to build customer relationships.

2.   Being a business partner that can be trusted.

3.   Providing timely responses to the sales and product inquiries.

4.   Offering the flexibility to buy in accordance with customer preference.

5.  Offering warranty terms and conditions that best meet the customers' needs.

6.  Having products and services available when the customer wants them.

7.  Having products that are easy to integrate with other industry standard products and services.

8.  Offering the most competitive initial price on hardware and services.

9.  Taking ultimate responsibility for service problems regardless of who provides the services.

10. Offering the most complete set of features and functionality to meet customer demands.

The **foregoing findings provided by the POR (PORI and CSI)**—and presented here in broad, general terms in order to exclude more detailed classified information—enable producers of Internet Personal Computer Products globally to set industry priorities and to proceed with both confidence and caution in regard to product improvement and the introduction of new technology.

Results from careful analysis of feedback obtained through the POR (PORI and CSI) also assisted **Compaq and the Subject Companies D, H and I** in composing a profile of items that need to be considered in order to appeal to customers who purchase Internet Products globally: **E-Commerce capabilities (now going paper-less), Services Marketing, Services Features and Benefits, Product Warranty, Warranty Management, Managed Services (U.S. or abroad), Configurable Warranty, On-Line Services, and the Internet Keyboard.**

**Also important** are: Electronic Credit Decision and Transaction Status, Electronic Delivery of pre-populated Lease Contract, Management from acceptance through end of Lease Decision, **Electronic Lease Acceptance by Customer**, Web **Shopping Integration** and **complete paper-less Leasing**, Service Marketing offering **Warranty extensions** that incrementally improve the service coverage of the Internet Computer Product, Hardware Services supporting critical service needs of the products most important to customer business, Software Services and Software Support of the day-to-day Business Applications, and Installation and **Start-up Services** ensuring ease of set-up and full functionality, right out of the box.

Changes Made in Response to Attribute Analysis Data in response to the kind of consumer feedback made possible through the POR (PORI and CSI), Compaq<sup>TM</sup> and the other Subject Companies D, H and I upgraded many service features and benefits in terms of quality and of specific customer demands. For example, such services and benefits are sold, shipped and stocked just like hardware, and customers only pay for the services and levels of service they truly need. These features and benefits are well integrated and supported in order to provide customers with a single point of contact convenient to there computing environments without the expense of maintaining an in-house technical staff.

These offers range from products to improve personal productivity to services that minimize hardware downtime in business-critical situations. Another area in which POR (PORI and CSI) feedback has resulted in adjustment and improvement is Product Warranty. Product Warranty Management requires that all SKUs (models) are identified reliable, and the warranty terms have been loaded into the warranty system application globally. The warranty metrics and glossary are finalized, ensuring flexibility to offer varying warranties by unit serial number, model and country or region. This results in the ability to vary default warranty to meet market needs and to have global redeemable warranty with varying warranty terms: **Configurable Warranties** and, 90-90-0, 1-1-0, 1-1-1, 3-1-0, 3-1-1 and 3-3-3 (numbers are in years). On-Line Services (OLS) are key to success in the global market, and this is another area in which the information provided by the **POR (PORI and CSI)** has been critical. Product launch targets coincide with OLS launch targets except in Norway, Denmark, Portugal and Australia because of Internet availability. To date, countries who have prioritized OLSs have indicated that some of their top ranking needs or demands will require some form of assistance from the targeted country, region or corporate. An example of the modifications and improvements that have been made in Internet Computer Products in order to accommodate a global market is the Internet Keyboard. The Internet Keyboard provides users not only with a fully functional keyboard but also with a complete Internet button suite which can enable them to begin to harness the power of the Internet immediately and with ease. The Internet button suite includes standard features, online mail, online community, online OEM information, online start, online search, online services, and online commerce. Enabling the Internet keyboard is done by keyboard buttons being coded to redirect URLs by country in the appropriate language. OLS teams/regions determine final URL destinations. If there is no final URL destination, a default Web Page template is selected and the OLS team will verify the final URL destination on redirector server. Currently available for effective rollout of Internet keyboard functionality is: United States, United Kingdom, France, Spain, Sweden, Belgium, Luxembourg and Canada as default URLs. Thus, each company (subject) surveyed can benefit in many categories.

# Review and Conclusion of POR

**What is the POR?** The POR along with its testing and assessment instruments (PORI and CSI) is a computer product strategic management information tool for producing IPC product (Internet Personal Computer products globally).

In July of 1999, an anonymous article in London's *The Economist* stated: "Though they [personal computer companies] will sell more machines in the next few years, 1999 may prove the high-water mark for revenues in the industry's American heartland. As for profits, even in today's market they are hard to come by—witness recent losses at Compaq™, the world's biggest PC maker. Although some of Compaq's difficulties are unique...few of its competitors are thriving either." The article goes on to point out, "These low profits partly reflect overcapacity and competition for market share. But PC makers are also worried that the relentless cycle of upgrades, stoked by marketing and technology, is losing steam. The main cause is the Internet, the very phenomenon that many believed would be their greatest opportunity" (Anonymous, 53). As analysts like Tricia Campbell, in her July 1999 article "Compaq tries to reboot," had already begun noting, "things weren't going so well for Compaq" (Campbell, 20). These were the industry conditions that motivated the author to propose developing the Plan of Record (POR, PORI and CSI), and they were the conditions that made Senior Management receptive to and enthusiastically supportive of that proposal. The general slump in PC sales and the new and mounting problems created by the Internet and coping with a global market called for immediate remedies, and so the approach to developing the POR was practical, no-nonsense, hands-on. The POR development and initial implementation were accomplished "in the field" and "on the job" where it was possible to determine post haste whether a feature of the plan or of its testing instruments was effective or not. As details in previous discussion have indicated, Compaq and the other Subject Companies began responding, likewise post haste, as the POR, PORI and CSI made information available. **It has been noted by October, 2000, Todd Wasserman gave attention to Compaq's changed policies with regard to Customer Services and Consumer Satisfaction** (expressed in his article, "'Customer view' defines Compaq's branding tack"); and by April 2001, Elana Harris devoted an article to

Compaq's dedication to "**Keeping customers happy.**" **Customer feedback** was accommodated in Planning and Design, and that influence became obvious as early as January 2000 when Walter S. Mossberg wrote, for the most part favorably, about the "**Quaint Old Look and Slick New Features**" of **Compaq's EZ 2200.** This influence is evidenced again when, in January 2001, Todd Wassetman **calls attention** to the fact that Compaq[TM] is marketing an IA (Internet Appliance), a slimmed-down, cable-free alternative to the PC, aimed primarily at senior citizens who have been intimidated by the complexity of a PC and random annoyances that the industry has failed to address ("PCs Unplugged," 24-27). Addressing the "random annoyances" is a reason for keeping the POR solidly in place. It can be re-emphasized, in conclusion, that the Plan of Record (**POR**) and its testing and assessment instruments, the Plan of Record Index (**PORI**) and Customer Satisfaction Index (**CSI**), **demonstrated success** in their initial implementation in that the companies involved **benefited measurably** from the information which these systems made available; **because of the looping-back feature of the POR**, those benefits should be ongoing. Conceivably the specifications of the POR and its related instruments PORI and CSI. of The POR could be as beneficial to other Internet Personal Computer Product companies as it is proving to be for Compaq[TM] and Subject Companies D, H and I. It is a tool/ Guide that can be utilized in bringing a degree of order and uniformity to a still very volatile industry by offering a means of achieving strategic product management and quality control.

# References

American Society for Quality Control. (1988) *AQC 42nd Annual Quality Congress Transactions*. Milwaukee, WI.

American Society for Quality Control. (1987) *Quality Systems—Model for Quality Assurance in Production and Installation*. Milwaukee, WI.

American Society for Quality Control. (1987). *Quality Management and Quality System Elements—Guidelines*. Milwaukee, WI.

Anonymous. Business: a bad business *The Economist* (1999, July 3). 352(8126) 53-54.

Amsden, Robert T., Howard E. Butler, and David M. Amsden. *SPC Simplified*. White Plains, NY: UNIPUB/Iraus International Publications,

Bailey, Holly. The Tech Effect: The Computer Industry's Increased Campaign Cost. *Computer Industry* (1999, Nov. 8), 5 (33) 1-3. http://www:opensecrets. Org/alerts/v5/alertv5.33asp

Barlas, Stephen. Manufacturing Quality. *Managing Automation*. (1996, March), 2, 61-74.

Bedeian, Arthur G. (1989). *Management*. 2nd Edition. New York: The Dryden Press.

Briody, Dan and Terho Uimonen. PC manufacturers await quake impacts, *Infoworks*. Framingham: (1999, Sept. 22), 71 (30), 8.

Butler, Howard E. and Robert T. Amsden. (1983). *SPC Simplified for Services: Practical Tools for Continuous Quality Improvement*. White Plains, N.Y.: Quality Resources.

Burrows, Peter. The Big Squeeze in the PC Market. *Business Week.* (1999, September 20), Industrial/technology Edition, 40-41.

Campbell, Tricia. Compaq tries to reboot. *Sales and Marketing Management.* (1999, July) <u>151</u> (7) 20-21.

Carlton, Jim, Deborah Solomon, Pui-Wilng Tam, Khanh T. I. Tran and Julia Angwin. Digits. *Wall Street Journal.* Eastern Edition. B6-7.

Costano, Anthony, Quality. *Journal* (1989, April), <u>4</u>, 27-28.

Daft, Richard L. (1991). *Management.* 2<sup>nd</sup> Edition. New York: The Dryden Press.

Dvorak, John C. The Computer Industry Slowdown *Net News.* (2001, January 3). 1-4. Wysiwyg://31/http://www.Ordernet.com/slowdown.shtml

_____ Have You Got Gremlins? *Net News* (2001, March), 1-3.

Faletra, Roberta. Is there no one willing to shake it up in this industry any longer? *Crn.: The Newsweekly for Builders of Technology Solutions.* (2001, May 7), Issue 944, 140.

Forman, Preston. Thin-client enthusiast expands business with simple solutions *Computer Reseller News.* (1999, March), Issue 833: 39, 42.

Freed, Les. Personal Computers: History and Development. (1995) *The History of Computers.* New York: Ziff-Davis.

Gaither, Norman. (1990). *Production and Operations Management.* 4<sup>th</sup> Edition. New York: The Dryden Press.

Gardner, Charles H. *Roadblocks on the Information Highway.* <u>http://super.nova.org/</u> *Stories/Roadblocks/S2.html*

Geisel, Larry E. Knowledge-Based CIM Support. *Journal of Manufacturing Systems,* (1995, Jan.) 62-4.

Gitlow, H. S. and S. J. Gitlow. (1987). *The Deming Guide to Quality and Competitive Position.* Englewood Cliffs: Prentice Hall, Inc.

Gold, Bela and Gene McCarroll. Towards the Increasing Integration of Management Functions: Needs and Illustrated Advances. *International Journal of Technology Management.* (1998), 10-20.

Guth, Robert A. and Evan Ramstad. How Sony Turned a Skinny Laptop Into an Unlikely PC Success. *Wall Street Journal.* (1999, Nov. 12). Eastern Edition. B, 1-2.

Hamilton, Anita. Tempting deal *Time.* (1999, Aug. 9),.154, (6), 75-76.

Hamilton, David P. and Dean Takahashi. PC Makers Worry About Memory Chip Shortage. *Wall Street Journal.* (1999, Oct. 4). Eastern Edition. B11-12.

Harris, Elana. Keeping customers happy. *Sales and Marketing Management.* (2001, April), 153 (4), 69-70.

Harvey, John and Gerald L. Page. *Journal: Harvard Business Review (HBR),* (1995, Feb.), 64. 69-76.

Hawkins, Del I., Roger J. Best, and Kenneth A. Coney. (1994). *Consumer Behavior.* 5th Edition. New York: Richard D. Irvin, Inc.

Hutchens, Spencer. Editorial. *Compliance Engineering.* (1991, Fall), 19.

*ISO International Standards for Quality Management.* (1987) ISO. Geneva, Switzerland.

Koehler, William. Production and Inventory Management *Manufacturing Journal.* (1993, May), 48, 44-49.

LaMorte, Christopher and John Lilly. *Computers: History and Development.* http://www.digitalcentury.com/encyclo/update/comp.hd:html

Mack, Ann M. Engage links marketing deal with Compaq. *Brandweek.* (2000, Sep. 18), 41 (30), 40-41.

McMaster, Mark. Making changes easy for salespeople. *Sales and Marketing Management.* (2001, Jan.) 153 (1), 74-75.

McWilliams, Gary. Shortages of an Intel Microprocessor Create Backlogs, Headaches. *Wall Street Journal.* (2000, *Aug. 13), 8.*

Mossberg, Walter S. Be on Your Guard For These 10 Lies As You Shop for a PC. *Wall Street Journal.* (2001, January 18), Eastern Edition, B1-2.

Mossberg, Walter S. Compaq's New Series Has a Quaint Old Look and Slick New Features. *Wall Street Journal.* (2000, Jan. 6), Eastern Edition. B1-3.

Munger, Michael. On the Flip Side: The Computer Industry is So Predictable *The Mac Observer.* (2000, April 11), 1-5. http://www:macobserver. com/columns/ Flipside/2000/20000411.shtml

Nance, Barry. Testing, testing…1, 2, 3. *Network World.* (2001, Feb.19), 18 (8), 50-51.

Phelps, Alan. Mainframe to Mainstream: Computers Make Their Way into Daily Life. *Computing Dictionary.* Third Edition. (1998, December) 2 (4), 1-11

Polsson, Ken. *Chronology of Personal Computers.* 1995–2001. URL http:// www.island Net.com/-kpolsson/comphist.

Process Management Institute. (1987). *Fundamentals of Process for Quality Assurance In Production and Installation.* Milwaukee, WI.

Process Management Institute. (1987). *Fundamentals of Process Improvement.* Bloomington, MN.: Process Management Institute.

Rise Of The 'Wintel Monopoly' The, Smart Computing Editorial., 1-11. http:// www.smartcomputing.com/editorial.

Robbins, Stephen P. (1991). *Organizational Behavior.* 5th Edition. New York: Prentice-Hall, Inc.

Sager, Ira. Bringing Mainframe Might to PC Servers, *Business Week.* (1999, July 5), Industrial/technology Edition. Issue 3636, 88.

Sandbert, Jared. Why Combo Gizmos Don't Cut It—TV-PCs, Web-Access Phones Show That Whole Can Be Less Than Sum of Its Parts. *Wall Street Journal.* (2001, April 25), Eastern Edition. B1-2.

Schonberger, Richard. (1991). *World Class Manufacturing Casebook: Implementing JIT and TQC.* 3rd Edition. New York: Free Press.

Surviving the Next Operating System: Dos RIP: 1981, 1990, 1993, 1995,…. *PC Operating Systems*. (1996, March 25), http://www.yale.edu/pelt/OPSYS/ Default.litm.

Thomas, Jason. Reactions by the Computer Industry to the World Wide Web. *Ethics And Law on the Electronic Frontier*. Fall, 1994. Papers/thomas-comp-industry. http://www.swiss at mit.edu/6805/student

Toupin, Laurie Ann. "Virtual Assembly Processes Come to the PC Screen." *Design News*. Apr. 18, 1999. Vol. 54, Issue 8, p. 18.

Tran, Khanh T. L. Microsoft, Nintendo Gear Up to Compete For Sales of Their Video-Game Consoles. *Wall Street Journal*. Eastern Edition. B8-9.

Wasserman, Todd. 'Customer view' defines Compaq's branding tack. *Brandweek*. (2000, October 9), 41 (39), 10-11.

_____. Textbook Notebook. *Brandweek*. (2001, Apr. 16), 42 (l6),. 28-20.

_____. PCs unplugged *Brandweek*. (2001, Jan. 1), 42 (1). 24-27.

_____. Softness Yields CE Focus for PC Bets, Microsoft Plans Two Lines Of Attack. *Brandweek*. (2001, Jan. 15), 42, (3), 14.

White, Stephen. *A Brief History of Computing*. 1996–2001. 1-3. http:// www.ox compsoc.net/-swhite/history: html

Zarley, Craig and Joseph F. Kovar. IBM Reaches Out. *Cm. : The Newsweekly For Builders of Technology Solutions*. (2001, Feb. 26), Issue 934: 14-18.

Zikmund, William G. (1992). *Business Research Methods*. 3rd Edition. New York: The Dryden Press.

# Special, Future Research On What's To Come…In The Computer Solutions Industry

A postmortem on Internet personal computer producers that resist this global utilized method **POR** within the global market place and current price wars, and the **real** concerns of more computer company mergers and acquisitions that eliminate knowledge because of **ego** and lose the gains and keep the loses. The reader needs to know that the **POR** and its elements **PORI/CSI** are also being utilized to successfully computer produce products and services for Small and Medium Business as well as Enterprise Class products and Services since the publication of this book. It also should be noted and is know that many computer/IT producers of hardware and software are outsourcing operations to other countries like: China/Taiwan and the Czech Republic facility, and so far the most cost effective countries are within the Eastern Europe block. Even with these strategic changes the **POR remains intact** as the business management tool being utilized.

**In summary**, New hidden markets are being found every day, for example within the next three year period the computing producers globally will focus their efforts and product offerings not only to you and I the consumer, but also toward the fastest growing market "Small & Medium market segment to date", "the Entertainment market segment", "the "Medical market segment", "Wireless technologies market segment", and "the Military market segment as well" for obvious reasons. After reading this book it is my hope that you the reader learned something that will help you in your decision making "choices"…

# QUESTIONS AND ANSWERS

## Question

What are the major elements of SPC and the advantages and disadvantages associated with its use? What is the role it plays in TQC?

## Answer

In reviewing your question and each of its parts in terms of its impact on the PC industry, In their book, *SPC Simplified*, outlines and clarifies the first of two systems that were devised in attempts to regulate and facilitate the production and marketing of the PC. The systems that these authors discuss are Statistical Process Control (SPC) and Total Quality Control (TQC). "Statistical Process Control (SPC) identifies three major elements of SPC. These elements are the Supplier, OEM and Customer elements" (Amsden & Butler, 100)." Each element has a specific expectation. The Supplier has the expectation of ensuring material quality improvement processes. These processes are accomplished, quality first, by identifying the need for and making changes to the methodology involved in assembling each piece part, and, second, by determining what its relevant piece part cost is to the next step in this process, which is the OEM. The OEM (Original Equipment Manufacturer) element has an expectation that encompasses the measurement of systems. This means that the OEM examines what the test requirements and design expectations of the product are and evaluates product fall-out (in manufacturing the units that do not pass the test). The Customer element has an expectation that the computer product manufacturer will meet Customer product standards. These standards were identified by general market (Customer) research that included Basic Form and Fit and Functionality of the product line. As they note, "Statistical Process Control (SPC) methods assist the planning and product management processes". While Statistical Process Control (SPC) worked to alleviate some of the problems in the PC industry, the system could not anticipate the rapid changes brought about by steadily increasing, ever more sophisticated technology. The manufacturing challenges were great as companies struggled to meet the demands of growing and often unexpected markets and of consumers who, unlike the first PC enthusiasts, were no longer willing to tolerate shortcomings and glitches and who were savvy enough to see possibilities that had not been realized and to demand that these be incorporated in their product. In an article titled "**Production Management**," published in April 1989 edition of *Quality*, Anthony Costanzo insisted, "Research is needed to understand and meet the larger market demands for a higher quality personal computer product" (Costanzo, 23). Computer companies struggled to meet this challenge. This new research produced an information technology strategic management marketing tool called Total Quality Control (TQC). Because SPC became increasingly inadequate in terms of complex industry demand, TQC was developed to augment it. It becomes clear that "quality" is intensified with SPC to create TQC.

**Shonberger, Richard**. (1991), World class manufacturing casebook: *Implementing JIT and TQC*. New York: Free Press. "The key items between SPC and TQC involve quality enhancement. Utilizing JIT (Just-In-Time) manufacturing to address piece part cost-to-build and deliver information as well as general customer service, TQC became a very effective computer product management information process tool in the early 1990s. The turning point for TQC came when the global market changed and computer products became Internet computer products for consumers as well as businesses worldwide".

# Question

What is project management and discuss the project management process associated with it?

# Answer

"Project management is the process of guiding your project from its beginning through its performance to its closure. Project management processes are defined as a series of actions designed to bring about specific results. There are five processes that should be applied to each phase of a project in order to bring about the completion of the phase: Initiating, Planning, Executing, Controlling and Closing" (Gray & Larson, 26).

*Initiating* means getting a project or project phase authorized. It involves obtaining the organization's commitment to the project as a whole. Typically, the sponsor, customer, or person providing the funds gives the authorization to begin a project or phase. So, in effect, initiating means getting the green light from the client (For me were Compaq senior management and Suppliers) to begin work on the project POR.

*Planning* is a major importance on a project because by definition the project involves creating something unique. In other words, you may be heading into un-charted waters, so you should have a plan to help you get through them safely. There are two types of planning: essential planning and discretionary planning. Essential planning consists of four sub processes: Defining the scope (all the products and services to be provided by the project), Identify or defining the required activities, resources, and schedule, creating detailed **cost estimates** and budgets and Integrating all above into a comprehensive project plan. Discretionary planning processes are desirable but not necessarily required to complete a project. These processes are performed as needed and included creation of formal plans such as: Quality plan, Communications plan, Staffing plan (over and above that described in the essential plan), Procurement plan, Risk assessment and response plan and other formal plans dictated by organizational values and polices.

**Executing** is the process by which project plans are carried out. Executing involves several sub processes: Project Plan Execution—carrying out the project plan as written, Team Development—developing individual and group skills to enhance project performance, Information Distribution—making needed information available to project stakeholders in a timely manner, Solicitation—obtaining quotations, bids, offers, or proposals from contractors or vendors, Source Selection—choosing from among potential contractors or vendors and Control Administration—managing the relationship with the contractor, vendor, including such activities as handling paperwork and ensuring payment.

*Controlling* involves comparing actual performance with planned performance. In other words, are you doing exactly what you planned to do? Controlling involves several sub processes: Progress Reporting—collecting and disseminating progress information to all project stakeholders, Overall Change Control—coordinating changes across the entire project, Scope Change Control—controlling changes to project scope, **Cost Control**—controlling changes to the project budget, Quality Control—monitoring specific project results to determine if they comply with relevant quality standards and identify ways to eliminate causes of unsatisfactory performance, Quality Assurance—evaluating overall project performance regularly to provide confidence that the project will satisfy the relevant quality standards and Risk Control—attempting to minimize the effect that unknowns are potential negative events will have on the project.

*Closing*—Because projects are temporary endeavors, projects and project phases must eventually come to an end. Closing involves formally accepting the results and ending the project or phase. This includes several sub processes: Scope Verification—ensuring that all identified project deliverables have been completely satisfied, Administrative Closure—generating, gathering, and disseminating information to formalize project completion, often including sign-off or written approval of the deliverables or phase and Contract Close-Out—completion and settlement of the contract, including resolution of any outstanding items.

# Question

What are the elements of strategic quality management? How do you identify the critical success factors? How do you use the critical path method? Are they related?

# Answer

In their book, Strategic Management, *Total Quality & Global Competition*, identifies and explains the elements of strategic quality management. As they note, "Elements of strategic management are Organization and Administration, Review Strategic Plans, Perform Financial Analysis, Review Operations (manufacturing, suppliers, engineering, marketing/sales, financial costs, personnel), Finalize Strategic Plans (document product plan, document marketing/sales plan, document manufacturing plans, document supplier plans, document organizational plan, document financial plan, and management review), Prioritize Strategic Opportunities, Plan implementation (immediate action) and Management Review" (Stahl & Grigsby, 9).

"**Critical success factors** are identified by changes in percentages of the critical path variables identified both dependent and independent" (Lockyer, Keith & Muhlemann, 421). The critical path method is used as the project is given a 'target' or 'acceptable' time. In this case the backward pass will start with the target time. Under these circumstances the critical path may itself have float (positive float if the target time is greater than the final E=figure, negative float if the target time is less than the final E=figure). Criticality is measured by the same size of the Float. The critical factors are related in that they both use an Activity, Start, Finish and Float principle.

# Question

Describe briefly the Six Sigma approach and give the five steps associated with it.

# Answer

"The Six Sigma approach can be described as representing a statistical measure and a management philosophy for improved quality." Sigma is like a measurement, used to determine how good or bad the performance of a process is; in other words, how many mistakes a company makes, doing whatever it does. The Six in Sigma is the level of perfection. The five steps associated with Six Sigma are to Define, Measure, Analyze, Improve and Control "(Chowdhury, Subir. 79). An example of an Six Sigma approach would be: Lets say your company's working at One Sigma. That means the company is making about 700,000 defects per million opportunities, or DPMO. This would be viewed according to the Six Sigma approach as doing things right about 30 percent of the time. Two Sigma is better. If your working at Two Sigma, you're making a little over 300,000 mistakes per million opportunities. Most companies operate between three and Four Sigma, which means they make between approximately 67,000 and 6,000 mistakes per million chances, respectively. If your operating at 3.8 Sigma, that means you're getting it right 99 percent of the time according to the Six Sigma approach. A one percent margin of error can add up to a lot of mistakes. When Six Sigma was created the quality goals were raised from Four Sigma to Five Sigma. Six Sigma has the perception of being a quality improvement approach, Pick one problem to solve at a time as a project. Reviewing Six Sigma from a management approach is that the Executive Leadership has to be the driving force behind adopting the Six Sigma philosophy and inspiring the organization from day one. A good CEO will likely appoint one of his executives to oversee and support the entire mission. This sends the signal to everyone that the company is serious. The Development Champions provide leadership and commitment and work to implement Six Sigma throughout their businesses. The Project Champion's job is to oversee, support, and fund the Six Sigma projects and personnel necessary to get the job done. This allows the people on the project to focus on the project at hand. The Master Black Belts are the people most responsible for creating lasting, fundamental changes in the way the company operates from top to bottom. The Black Belts are the people who really do the work. They're the key to the whole project, the true leaders of Six Sigma. The Green Belts provide the Black Belts the support they need to get the project done. The main thrust of Six Sigma is to reduce errors and waste in every kind of business endeavor to please customers and fatten the bottom line.

# Question

What is a process quality audit and what roles does it play in continuous improvement?

# Answer

Keith Lockyer, "Production and Operations Management: Conformance Quality, (1988), a Chapter in his book, notes that "A process quality audit checks the quality system is functioning satisfactorily. The role quality audit process plays in is continuous improvement by checking the quality system in terms of recording and analysis of data in this aspect of quality and it is here that the tools of SPC must be applied effectively". The Quality Audit is part of the Conformance Quality design of which other elements are measured as well. Some of these elements can be Internal failure costs, Scrap, Rework, Re-inspection, Downgrading, Failure analysis, External failure costs, Repair, Warranty costs, Complaints, Returns, Liability, Appraisal costs, Inspection and test, Inspection equipment, Vendor rating, Prevention costs, Product requirements, Quality planning, Quality assurance, Training and Miscellaneous activities.

# Question

List the main goals and objectives for implementing the system engineering process in the design and development of a product. What can this process contribute to product innovation? How, can this impact the cycle time?

# Answer

In the book, Quality Management System, (1988), outlines and clarifies the main goals and objectives of implementing the system engineering process in the design and development of a product and that is "the design is the translation of requirements into a form suitable for production or use. It may include redesign to cater for ease of production or change in specification and in terms of development, there is improvement of existing techniques, ideas or systems" (Willborn, Walter, 25). This process of system engineering contributes to production innovation by providing strategic information into the design of the project: Conception, Acceptance, Execution, Translation and Pre-operations. The system engineering process can impact Cycle time (C) by the time available at each station for the performance of the work allocated to it. C is obtained from the demand: C=T/Q. The layout of workstations, Product layout: Line balancing and total work content are a few processes that are associated with cycle time.

# *ABOUT THE AUTHOR*

I've lived in both Northern California (San Francisco, Mountain View), and Southern California (Los Angelas, Woodland Hills, Canoga Park, and Santa Ana).

Today my home is deep in the heart of South Central Texas (Houston). I've been fortunate to travel all over the world, working with many companies, suppliers, vendor's, getting to know the unique business cultures, the people, and different technologies that are being utilized yesterday, today and into the future. This opportunity continues to be simply amazing and a tremendous learning experience.

For example, some companies use SPC and a some suppliers use Six Sigma for their process controls, it's a mix...What stood out, clear as a Bell, was that both these processes were their own separate entities and alike in many ways, not really being utilized as part of an entire plan from concept through development, and where was the customers input? Some folks refer to this as "THE-BIG-PIC-TURE."

During the POR research/study, and its creation, Wayne Holovacs, MBA, BS was a Senior Manager/Executive of Staff. "Dr. Wayne", earned his Ph.D., in Business Management (Engineering, Management dissertation, implemented by Compaq).

Dr. Wayne also achieved an MBA in Information Systems, and a BS in Marketing/Production earlier in his career. Up and until then, It was a humbling moment to see that the POR would become the "BIG-PICTURE" a new management information technology, called POR.

Dr. Wayne's part is as author and Team Leader of The POR (PORI and CSI), while with Compaq Computer Corporation$^{TM}$.

Detailed global work experience portfolio of more than 16 years as a hands-on Senior Manager/Director of Staff responsible for engineering, technical and administrative duties of each global product and services division within Compaq Computer Corporation (Consumer, Small & Medium Business, Commercial, Enterprise Class, and External Storage SAN/NAS engineering development teams.

A few additional accomplishments include the delivery of more than 100+ global products and services of all types of new Computing and Enterprise Digital Imaging technologies to our customers and within these industries worldwide. Dr. Wayne was also assigned Executive Liaison, and the Product and Services Global Manager, to assist in the global merger and acquisition of both the Digital Equipment Corporation (DEC$^{TM}$) merger, and also with the Hewlett Packard Corporation$^{TM}$ global acquisition of Product and Services Development within the Enterprise Class SAN/NAS global business division.

Dr. Wayne is recognized for "Outstanding Achievement" as development and launch Manager of the Microsoft$^{TM}$ Data Center Services technology in 2000.

Dr. Wayne is a co-creator, teacher and former Core Member of the NEW global *Interoperability* Standards for External Enterprise Storage Technologies SAN/NAS (hardware/software, Testing, Services and Support).

Is a former Board Member of Storage Network International Association (SNIA), 2001. *Duties as Board Member:*

Interaction and representation for numerous Enterprise Class Suppliers$^{TM}$/Vendors$^{TM}$ globally, as well as Compaq Computer Corporation$^{TM}$.

Other work assignments included Regional Manager of Technical Support and Services for Intergraph Corporation$^{TM}$ the leader in Digital Graphics design and Imaging company, as product and services leader worldwide being part of the Services Division. Providing Services and Technical Support to Intergraph Clients/Customers within the Computer/Enterprise Class, and Digital Imaging industry.

In closing what helped our team the most in terms of "work-ethic" was to have a "coach like, work ethic", all on the same team, yet we are each individual contributors all…

"I am known around the world in the industries mentioned as "***Dr. Wayne***".

0-595-29886-9